EXPERT LEGAL WRITING

Expert Legal Writing

Terri LeClercq

Foreword by
Chief Justice Thomas R. Phillips
Supreme Court of Texas

 University of Texas Press, Austin

Third paperback printing, 2000

Requests for permission to reproduce material from this work should be sent to Permissions, University of Texas Press, Box 7819, Austin, TX 78713-7819.

ⓧ The paper used in this publication meets the minimum requirements of American National Standard for Information Sciences—Permanence of Paper for Printed Library Materials, ANSI Z39.48-1984.

Library of Congress Cataloging-in-Publication Data
LeClercq, Terri, date.
    Expert legal writing / Terri LeClercq.
      p.   cm.
    Includes bibliographical references and index.
    ISBN 0-292-74687-3 (hardcover : acid-free paper). —
  ISBN 0-292-74688-1 (pbk. : acid-free paper)
     1. Legal composition. 2. Law—United States—Language.
  I. Title.
  KF250.L39   1995
808'.06634—dc20   95-6449

For Desiree, Noel, Glenn, and especially Jack

CONTENTS

FOREWORD

Lawyers, like salesmen, exist to communicate. The product lawyers sell is explaining, recording, and persuading about important matters in the lives of their clients. All good lawyers are communications experts.

In the ten years that Terri LeClercq has written about communication in the *Texas Bar Journal*, she has persuaded many of us that attention to prose style is just as important as attention to legal doctrine. Through these essays she explains and justifies the concrete rules of language and then takes us into the arena beyond rules: to the options for creating persuasive and memorable prose.

Dr. LeClercq reminds us that most lawyers, Perry Mason and Court TV notwithstanding, do their most important communication through the written word. The heart of most lawyers' work comes not in a rousing jury summation, but in the daily preparation of a ground lease, or an SEC S-3, or a routine request for production of documents. It is during this day-to-day writing that all of us can sharpen our writing skills by focusing on technique and the impact of our words.

As we all know, daily writing can all too easily become formulaic, boring, and careless. Our clients don't usually take the time to explain where we have failed them in this, but Dr. LeClercq does—she examines a variety of legal documents produced in law firms, state agencies, and, yes, our courts. She responds not as a rule-bound English teacher hunting for the passive voice, but rather as an interested advisor who will take the time to point out confusion and ambiguity. Attorneys who read this book will benefit from both her conclusions and her suggestions.

Dr. LeClercq has studied about and taught writing skills for twenty-five years, including ten years at The University of Texas School of Law. She has learned that legal writing is a skill that needs attention and work, including work by those of us who are out of law school. We all have something to learn.

This collection of essays has practical advice for every practicing attorney. From grammar and punctuation rules to sentence and organization suggestions, Dr. LeClercq demands practice, practice, practice—not just to improve the document at hand, but to make the lawyer a better communicator throughout his or her career. A poorly phrased clause in a will or contract may seem innocuous when it is drafted, but it can become critical later if the matter ends up in court, where even the most brilliant legal insights can be totally negated by bad writing.

The good advice in *Expert Legal Writing* is parceled out in short and concise chapters full of analogies and examples from a wide spectrum of legal fields. Whether it is read cover to cover or kept at hand for reference, every legal writer can benefit from this practical advice.

Better writing makes better lawyering, which improves the administration of justice for all of us.

Thomas R. Phillips
CHIEF JUSTICE
SUPREME COURT OF TEXAS

ACKNOWLEDGMENTS

Kelley Jones, Melinda Smith, and Ginger Banks of the *Texas Bar Journal* originally published these essays beginning in 1985; they and others on the Texas State Bar staff encouraged me to publish them as a book. With the help of the University of Texas School of Law, Professor Christy McCrary, Margaret Francis (secretary), Marlyn Robinson and David Gunn (U.T. law librarians), and Jacqueline Sandoval and Karen Spole (research assistants), those essays were incorporated and improved. I am thankful also to the many attorneys who invited me into their law firms, state agencies, and courts and who shared their expertise with me:

        Advocacy, Inc.
        Arnold, White & Durkee
        Bracewell & Patterson
        Brown & Maroney
        Cooper Industries
        Court of Appeals for the First District
        Cox & Smith
        Groce, Locke & Hebron
        Haynes and Boone
        Hoover, Bax & Shearer
        McCauley, MacDonald, Love & Devin
        Mayer, Brown & Platt
        Office of Court Administration

Office of General Counsel, University of Texas
Office of the Attorney General of Texas
Panhandle Eastern Petroleum Company
Phillips Petroleum Company
Public Utility Commission of Texas
Shannon, Gracy, Ratliff & Miller
Small, Craig & Werkenthin
StarEnterprises
State Bar of Texas
State Comptroller of Public Accounting
State Department of Banking
Supreme Court of Texas
Tarrant County Women's Bar Association
Texas Eastern Transmission Company
Texas Employment Commission
Texas Railroad Commission
Texas Senate Staff

I
INTRODUCTION
Getting and Keeping a Competitive Edge

You cannot improve your body structure or stamina just by listening to an expert describe exercise techniques.

You cannot improve your writing style just by listening to an expert describe prose techniques.

INTRODUCTION

Working on writing skills is painful—painful to think about, to procrastinate about, to actually attempt, and to evaluate. That pain resembles the pain of first taking an exercise class, and all the familiar excuses work for both activities.

SIMILAR EXCUSES FOR NOT EXERCISING

- I don't have time to stop and exercise.

- No one is complaining, so I must look OK for my age.

- I don't need an exercise class; I can do it on my own.

- I hate to start exercise class because everyone there is in better shape or is younger.

- I don't have the money to join a gym, hire a personal trainer, or buy how-to books.

- It'll hurt.

- I have too much to say and can't stop to focus on *how* I'm going to say it.

- The motions get filed, the clients pay their bills, so I must be an adequate writer.

- I don't need someone telling me how to write; all I have to do is write a little more often.

- I hate to attend writing seminars where everyone else is already published or knows what a "gerund" is.

- I don't have the money to go to a CLE course, hire an editor, or buy grammar books.

- It'll hurt.

SIMILAR MOTIVATIONS FOR BEGINNING TO EXERCISE

- It's been too long since I worked out.
- Someone comments on flab.

- Someone else looks a whole lot healthier or fits into clothes better.
- I have a special event (homecoming, wedding, speech) coming soon and need to look good.

- I used to look so cute.

- I haven't had any feedback on just my writing in years.
- Someone describes your writing as wordy, rambling.
- Other legal writers have more frequent success in court and with their clients.
- My (new job, new boss, or upcoming brief before a hostile judge) requires special attention to my prose.
- People used to compliment my writing, but it's been years since anyone has mentioned anything positive.

▬▬▬

Reading about physical exercise doesn't do the reader much good, and neither does reading about writing techniques, because physical muscles and mental gray matter can't grow without stimulus. Stimulus causes movement, so if it's time for you to move, to improve your prose style, why not follow the stimulating advice of the gurus of the exercise world who have changed the bodies and lives of so many exercisers.

HOW TO BEGIN

The most important thing to remember is that no one activity is a cure-all, no one activity will do everything for everyone. Picking an approach depends entirely on who you are and what you want from your fitness training. Each activity offers its own gains and has its own problems. . . . You can match your goals to a fitness approach that will enable you to achieve them.[1]

How you begin to concentrate on your writing is an individual choice. Some writers sign up for a review class. Others read books, like this one, to learn writing techniques they'll use in practice. Many read

▬▬▬

[1] JAMES GARRICK, BE YOUR OWN PERSONAL TRAINER 74 (1989).

good literature and emulate sentences and techniques from that reading. Still others spend time reviewing their own work to discover their own patterns and then decide what needs work next. Whatever the method, a decision to concentrate on the writing of a document instead of only on the content of a document requires an active decision to take the time to improve. Most experts agree that your time is best spent if it is focused on an articulated, attainable goal. If you want to improve your style, articulate a specific goal and decide how to reach it.

> Before you start a program of self-improvement, you need to isolate your problems. In addition to knowing your problems, you must have some idea of where you are going—an objective. You need short-term goals as well as long-term goals, even if they're only simple ones.[2]

> Virtually all successful body builders are extremely goal-oriented individuals, and it's difficult to accomplish any challenging task without the ability to set long-range goals, break them down into short-range goals, and pursue each goal with single-minded determination and maximum energy.[3]

> Herschel Walker offers advice to young athletes:

> I believe *variety* is best, because I think every time you play basketball you're working on skills that can help you play football, and every time you do karate you learn something that can help you in your other sports, and so on down the line. I even believe you can get better in sports by dancing. If you think about what you're doing, *any* kind of movement can help you learn about lots of other kinds of movement.[4]

Any practice in writing can help your legal writing. Write a complaint to your mechanic and spend some time editing it; read an essay from *Time* and, substituting your own topic, mimic the prose. Read a short chapter from a stylebook[5] that examines one element of style

---

[2] Jan Percival et al., The Complete Guide to Total Fitness 36 (1977).
[3] Rachel McLish, Flex Appeal 3–4 (1984).
[4] Herschel Walker & Terry Todd, Herschel Walker's Basic Training 5 (1985).
[5] See, e.g., Tom Goldstein & Jethro K. Lieberman, The Lawyer's Guide to Writing Well (1989); C. Edward Goode, Mightier than the Sword (1989); Joseph Williams, Style: Ten Lessons in Style & Grace (1981).

and then spend some time reviewing your documents, looking only at that particular element of style. Any of these activities involves you in the conscious evaluation of prose rather than content, and any of them can help you develop your own prose style.

> Visualize. . . . When you have fixed in your mind the image of the changed you, let that be your incentive for training and working out. This mental image should be your motivator, your goal, the ideal you are *determined* to reach. . . . After you have isolated the specific things you want to change, you must create willpower to carry through your desire. . . . Gradually, as you begin to see and feel results from exercise, maintaining your willpower will become easier.[6]

What is your goal? What would it mean, to you, to be a better writer? Perhaps "better writer" implies you would be able to characterize an argument or personality with only a few words; great writers can choose a few effective words to replace paragraphs of drafted ideas. Or perhaps being a "better writer" for you is being known throughout the city as a great brief writer. Occasionally I conjure up the image of John P. Frank's office wall in Phoenix which holds separate pictures of U.S. Supreme Court Justices. Several of them are inscribed: "To John P. Frank, a great writer!" I admit I fantasize about those inscriptions on my wall! What will you change about your style or your work habits to reach a height like that? Go for it.

Judi Sheppard Moffit, on trying to learn an aerobic move when she was eight:

> It was very frustrating. My back would arch when it shouldn't, my legs kicked too far apart, and the move seldom looked like it should.
>
> Fortunately, my instructor helped me break it down. She suggested that I concentrate on one element at a time and perfect it before I moved on to the next. . . . By the time the contest rolled around, I had mastered much more than the butterfly. I had learned how to break down a goal and concentrate on accomplishing one step at a time.[7]

---

[6] ARNOLD SCHWARZENEGGER, ARNOLD'S BODYSHAPING FOR WOMEN 31 (1979).
[7] JUDI S. MOFFIT, THE JAZZERCIZE WORKOUT BOOK 6 (1986).

Rather than embarking on a global reformation to "become a better writer," it will be helpful if you pinpoint one short-term goal and break down the steps it will take to reach that goal. If your goal is to be more succinct, for instance, try daily for one week to reduce each document by a half page. Another week, substitute stronger verbs to replace wordy noun clusters and adjectives. Then compare your old documents with these conscious writings and determine your progress.

A second aspect of Moffit's advice is equally useful: she received advice, feedback, from a professional. Perhaps another experienced attorney can read a few samples of your writing and offer you some seasoned advice. Perhaps a nonlegal friend can read your document and let you know if you communicated to the lay audience. Perhaps a writing professional can evaluate your prose and suggest techniques for improvement. It is difficult to know how to improve your prose until someone helps you pinpoint the problem. After that, like Moffit, you're on your own to develop the twists and turns that make you successful.

Afterward, of course, you'll want someone to read your prose again and offer yet another suggestion that you can begin to apply.

> You can start exercising with your morning shower . . . bend, stretch . . . walk to and from work, use the stairs . . . use television time for stretches, push-ups, lightweight dumbbells . . . park far from store entrance, push the lawnmower.[8]

Not all work on your writing has to be accomplished at the moment of writing a major brief or crucial letter; indeed, the real work and real progress will occur through daily, deliberate, repeated experiments with technique. Revise your standard letter format. Evaluate the style of your pleadings. When you read during the day, you can make it a point to consciously notice other writers' sparkling prose in magazines, newspapers, and perhaps even in other legal writing; you can learn from it right then. Right then is a great time to experiment with your own writing rather than waiting until you can formally attend a writing seminar or when you have "extra" time. Your daily writing tasks then become mini-lessons to reinforce writing skills.

▬▬▬

[8] *Shaping Up the (Almost) Painless Way,* EBONY, July 1992, at 38. See also Cheryl Sacra, *Same Job, Less Stress,* REDBOOK, Mar. 1993, at 40 (don't wait until you get home to unwind . . . take a mental vacation . . . shoulder circles and up-and-down head turns, foot rotations, arm raises at the desk); Carol Straley, *After the Baby Body Makeover,* PARENTS' MAGAZINE, Mar. 1990, at 147 (daily walking, floor exercises, using light weights).

The most unfortunate thing is that busy people equate their life styles with being physically active. They also equate their two rounds of golf a week with a means of maintaining good physical condition. This attitude is most unfortunate because we need some form of exercise to replace our lack of activity in order to avoid hypokinetic disease [a host of ailments].[9]

Just writing, by itself, is not a writing exercise. If you can visualize the reams of paper you produce in a month, you might think you've practiced so much that you're already a pro and don't need additional practice. But more writing is not better writing, as you know from reading the stacks of material that make their way to your desk.

Filling in routine pleadings and signing form letters are also not writing practice. Don't kid yourself. To work on your writing means to concentrate on it, to change it, to become a more effective communicator. Filing one more fill-in-the-blank pleading should not take the place of real exercise.

ADVICE ABOUT EXERCISE

You should enjoy your run—don't make it a chore or you're less likely to stick to it.[10]

Only 3 percent of all people who start exercise programs continue for a long time.[11]

Pick a short-term goal that appeals to you, e.g., snappy introductions to memoranda, and keep a file of your introductions. As you write and file, you'll begin to understand what you can, and can't, do with introductions. Make it a moment of self-affirmation to choose the most effective introduction of the month.

Then turn to another goal, some other aspect of writing that you want to work on. Really want it! If you want to become a more persuasive writer, review persuasive speeches or read editorials. Try out the technique you learn when writing your next argument, and sit back to enjoy the results!

■■■

[9] Charles Kuntzleman, The Exerciser's Handbook 5 (1978).
[10] Bob Delmonteque, Lifetime Fitness: How to Look Great at Any Age 64 (1993).
[11] Suzy Pruden, Change Your Mind, Change Your Body 2 (1992).

You're trying to change yourself gradually and painlessly, so don't try to be too good too soon. That usually leads to dropping out.[12]

If you believe you need to be as good a writer as your most successful legal opponents, and by tomorrow, you will have failed before you began. Why not define a short-term goal (e.g., stronger verbs) that will take you one step closer? Then you can celebrate the success of one step that is also leading toward a larger goal. If you set too tight a timetable for a too-miraculous improvement, you will undoubtedly become too guilty about breaking that schedule and quit altogether.

Early responses form our self images. . . . By high school most girls are unhappy with their bodies.[13]

Too many attorneys consider themselves "bad" writers. It defies logic that five attorneys in a ten-attorney office could each be labeled the worst writer there. These low self-images are self-defeating, keeping writers from giving their best efforts. Many participants in a writing course, for instance, label themselves "terrible" writers, even though the reality is that they are perfectly adequate. It may be that these insecure writers were victims of overly judgmental bosses or teachers. However it got there, this self-defeating image is difficult to change if the writers do not acknowledge and examine themselves. Given the technical difficulty of legal writing, the abstract nature of the law, and the need for references to precedent, little legal writing resembles Ernest Hemingway's terse prose. So get real about your field and the limitations inherent in it.

Since almost none of us is able to live up to these internalized, unrealistic standards, we hate ourselves and feel guilty and depressed. . . . [T]he goal of exercising and becoming fit is not to form yourself to the contours of some 'fashionable' mold, not to look like someone else, but to make your own body as vibrant and healthy as it can be, to affirm your own uniqueness.[14]

---

[12] JACKI SORENSEN, AEROBIC LIFESTYLE BOOK 18 (1983).

[13] THE MELPOMENE INSTITUTE FOR WOMEN'S HEALTH RESEARCH, THE BODY-WISE WOMAN 29, 41 (1990).

[14] JANE FONDA, JANE FONDA'S NEW WORKOUT AND WEIGHT-LOSS PROGRAM 11 (1986).

Within every law firm or agency is that "golden writer," someone who appears to be able to simultaneously research, draft, and polish every gem he or she produces. We all want to be that "golden one." Unfortunately, setting such an unattainable goal can stop anyone's progress. For instance, despite the pleasure of reading the words of a master writer, it's nevertheless destructive to expect yourself to perform to that level with every writing assignment. Similarly, although it's helpful to evaluate your boss's writing style (and avoid her pet peeves), it's unrealistic to believe you can duplicate the rhythm, the speed, and the style of her prose. By evaluating, you can improve, of course, but you cannot duplicate. A first step toward a realistic standard for your own prose should probably be to identify and label your own style—you have to have one, just as everyone has to have a personality. After that, you can decide how to improve on what is already there—your special flourishes, your trademark vocabulary, your pithy conclusions. Once you have begun to understand your own style, you will develop power from your prose ability, a power that allows you to trust your impulses when you try a different technique.

> Don't overdo—you are not competing with anyone. A competitive spirit just adds undesirable tension and stress.[15]

Attorneys have trouble following this bit of advice! You are already competing with the other side's legal counsel; you are competing against case precedent that leans to the other side's argument; you constantly compete against deadlines; and you are even competing, consciously or unconsciously, with other members of your own firm. Why add to this dizzying competition by bringing your writing style into the fray?

For those with enough competitions in their lives, I suggest you set your own realistic goals and then adjust those personal goals to your time schedule and varying audiences. That's enough. Don't try to compete with writers who have more experience; learn from them instead. For example, because I have created student handouts for the last twenty-five years, I can dream them up, prepare them, and have them ready faster and more efficiently than first-year teachers can. But I can't create children's poems faster and better than experienced poets. All I can hope is that by reading their poetry and questioning my own drafts,

---

[15] Jane Boutelle & Iamm S. Baker, Lifetime Fitness for Women 32 (1978).

I can painstakingly craft a poem that seems effortless to the reader. That's enough.

WHEN TO EXERCISE

> Three 10-minute exercise sessions spread throughout the day appear to do as much good for you as one 30-minute session.[16]

Attending to a writing exercise during one seminar is less useful than editing a draft in the morning and working on smooth transitions later in the day. Especially useful is a macroedit after finishing a draft, when you have more freedom to move large sections around, and a microedit the next day, when you can, for instance, choose more vibrant verbs and shorten sentences. Being conscious of style at different stages of the writing process can produce a stronger document than merely proofreading before sending it out.

> You should pick an aerobic activity that really interests you—one that you will stick with indefinitely—perhaps for the rest of your life. . . .
>
> . . . .
>
> Finally, after you've decided on your basic aerobic exercise, you should schedule a definite program for pursuing that activity and commit yourself to it for *at least 6 weeks.*[17]

Choosing to accomplish a particular writing goal may seem awkward at first, and of course time consuming, but repeated practice will pay off. A hit-or-miss approach to improved writing will only occasionally improve writing. That won't meet your long-term goal of developing into a golden writer. So, although it is unrealistic to believe you can focus specifically on writing style rather than on substance every day for six weeks, nevertheless your greatest success will follow a systematic course through the process of writing. Don't give up without giving the process time to work!

---

[16] JIMMY CONNORS, DON'T COUNT YOURSELF OUT: STAYING FIT AFTER 35, at 54 (1992).
[17] KENNETH COOPER, THE AEROBICS PROGRAM FOR TOTAL WELL-BEING 121 (1982).

You need exercise. No matter what your condition. Everyone does. Without exercise your body becomes sluggish—fat. The simple fact is you never graduate from the school of physical conditioning. . . . [T]he benefits of exercise cannot be stored for any great length of time.[18]

To tell yourself that you have already had a writing course (maybe back in law school) does not change the reality that you are not writing to your capability. You can improve, and should improve, with practice. Just writing on the job five hours a day, without concentrating on the *how* instead of the *what*, is not writing practice. You're just writing. You aren't learning, aren't growing, aren't staying competitive.

Many attorneys believe that any concentration on style is too time consuming. True, writing well simply is time consuming, but conscious, consistent practice can eventually make good writing easier and finally maybe even faster. At first, unfamiliar exercises are hard, are frustrating, and take lots of time. When they become familiar and automatic, they take less energy and time and produce more effective prose.

None of us writes as well as we would like. We're all on that journey to perfection—just on different steps. Learning to organize memoranda in law school, for instance, does not mean you will always know how to organize a legal discussion. Somewhere along the line, you need to concentrate again on organization, this time perhaps looking at topic sentences or perhaps concentrating on dovetailing transitions. These skills cannot be learned all at once, but they always lose importance when you have to focus on substantive arguments or when you have to make a deadline. Between crises, though, keep learning, keep practicing.

It's easy to give up, I know that. It's easy to throw a book like this across the room. . . . It's easy to give in to excuses and that little voice inside you that says it's hopeless.

However, the best things in life aren't easy. It's hard to get down on your mat each day; it's hard to do those push-ups and those sit-ups. But, honest to God, you can do it. I did it. I know you can.[19]

Few writers want to practice, want to spend time evaluating their prose instead of sending out the document and moving on to the

---

[18] CHARLES KUNTZLEMAN, THE EXERCISER'S HANDBOOK 3, 6 (1978).
[19] RICHARD SIMMONS, RICHARD SIMMONS' BETTER BODY BOOK 2 (1983).

next project. Most of us don't even want to proofread—and that's simple mechanics. To reread drafts and add transitions and move paragraphs and add headings and eliminate surplus words is tough and exhausting. Naturally, it's tempting to skip all the editing and think, "Well, they'll know what I meant to say." But the truth is that every assignment sent out without some conscious stylistic revision is an opportunity missed, a muscle that will continue to atrophy because we were too lazy or self-defeated to change. Perhaps this editing won't make a difference in that particular document, but the exercised muscle will make your prose style stronger for the next assignment, and the next.

CONCLUSION

No one can exercise for you. An instructor can help inspire you and direct you, but you have to fight through every self-improvement step yourself. The attorney who asks his office partner to "take notes at the writing seminar for me" obviously isn't going to get as much out of the notes as the participant did by listening to and following the exercises from an expert. Similarly, just reading about writing doesn't automatically make you a more efficient writer. You have to consistently apply what you've read. Even writing more often, but writing without feedback, will only get you more, but not better, written.

So it's back to the scratch pad or computer for all of us. Once the substantive ideas are drafted, the real work begins. And although we may hate to concentrate on rhetoric and process, we all love that marvelous surety of having written, and written well. This book is meant as a stimulus for those legal writers who already write well enough but want to write their best.

Can you remember the last brief you read that you found interesting and persuasive? Attorneys frequently plow through reams of dull, repetitive legal material and think: "Well, that's what I'm getting paid for. No one said my work would always be interesting."

1

WRITING LIKE A LAWYER

What does an English professor have to offer an experienced attorney? I think attorneys, experts in their substantive areas, can profit from considering a different perspective. Law students spend three years learning to think like a lawyer and the rest of their lives learning to act like one. Writing like a lawyer evolves mysteriously within that process but all too frequently with no overriding perspective, no formal instruction, and no constructive feedback. It's not just basic errors in English that keep legal writers from effectively and concisely communicating with clients and each other. Instead, it's a lack of awareness of audience—that person out there who is the intended recipient of the words you are struggling with. That's when a new perspective can come to your aid.

As an English professor, I've spent twenty-five years investigating the mystery of writing: what prose habits work and why. I read others' writings not to find the flaw within the argument but to analyze its effectiveness: Does this paper convince me of a point of view? Why or why not? Years of investigation have produced that distance from the material that allows me to judge and to teach both law students and experienced attorneys how to improve their written communication.

Some law firms use lawyers to teach legal writing. They teach the law, the process of research, the expediency of legal forms—but they rarely know how to explain why a sentence is "awkward" or why a memorandum is too dense. They are uncomfortable with "tone," "style," and "internal cues." Teaching writing to a practicing attorney takes patience on the part of the teacher and a belief in a busy attorney's ability to correct and polish style. Not many practicing attorneys have that time and optimism to share with their colleagues.

Within the law firm, partners necessarily help associates with their written communication. But the style preferred differs from partner to partner, from section to section of the firm. The emphasis can slip from clear communication to the writing habits of the supervising partner. Few associates are going to argue with a partner's suggestions, naturally, so the firm becomes locked into habits that may not produce the most effective communication.

What struck me as strange when I first began talking with attorneys about their writing was that their reactions to legal writing are only slightly different from a lay person's: they also find it too dense and unreadable. How excited are you to read a memorandum of law that your associate, or your opponent, has prepared?

No one made a rule that attorneys have to bore each other to death with a writing style tainted by archaic language. Sure, most legal documents have to follow the conventions of formal writing. But even in formal writing, an attorney can use crisp prose, short sentences, identifiable topic sentences. Writers who deliberately allow the time can polish the document and include metaphors, parallel ideas within parallel grammatical structures, introductions and summaries that persuade as well as inform.

And that's what this book is about.

Now can be the time to emphasize your own clear writing. Allot yourself a final half hour to read through your drafts—with a little fresh advice to spur you on. Before you know it, you may hear from a client who actually understands your latest letter or find a judge who takes home your brief because he is so interested in your argument that he wants to finish reading it before he goes to bed.

The improvement of your writing style will take a little work on my part and lots of work on yours. Welcome to an English professor's perspective.

2

WRITING'S A TOUCHY SUBJECT

Critics are always saying that legal writing is terrible, that lawyers simply cannot write. Surely the blanket condemnation cannot be *all* true in a profession that involves highly educated and intelligent people. What causes that perception, then—bad press?

Legal writers have four characteristics more or less in common that contribute to difficult-to-read documents. Those characteristics combine to create the image. First, what lawyers write is usually complicated. It's not as if you were filling in blanks at a bank. What you write is a concrete discussion of an abstract concept. That's difficult writing.

A second reason for troubled writing is time constraints. You have too much to do, and in too little time. That time crunch forces you to resort to submitting a first draft as a final draft.

Third, some attorneys haven't had a writing class since the seventh grade when they were placed in advanced English courses. I've quit being surprised at the number of expert attorneys who admit they haven't "had" to take a writing class since they were twelve years old. Since then the majority have been running on sheer native intelligence— no wonder a few of you have missed a subtle point or two in grammar and organization.

The fourth possible cause of bad legal writing is the one I want to concentrate on: familiarity. You write so much that you no longer see it as a challenge. It's hard for you to take pride in any particular document because you have so many others to complete: it's more important to get them done than to get them right.

When you write all day, as most of you do, you may get complacent and then perhaps sloppy. Using an analogy, I'm going to highlight one major problem and then offer some solutions.

One of the many gifts we take for granted is the sense of touch. Think for a minute about your spouse, POSSLQ (person of opposite sex sharing living quarters), or significant other. And think what it feels like to touch that person. Now, some of us are old enough to have touched so much that we no longer experience it very directly. That creates an interesting question of semantics: we've touched so much that we don't feel. Nevertheless, by some nefarious, diabolical quirk in human nature, even old experienced hands can feel when they touch—if what the hands touch is unexpected or especially appealing. A hand reaches out and bang! It's no longer metacarpals touching epidermis. It's electricity.

How can we, as rational, intelligent, educated people, explain this phenomenon? The skin of the significant other is familiar, and we take it for granted. Only by conscious determination can we resurrect the old excitement.

That's what I'm saying about your professional writing, too.

Drafting pleadings and in-house memoranda can become routine. In the pressure of day-to-day practice, attorneys lose their sense of wonder. The electricity dwindles, sputters, dies. But you can remember the first brief you worked on—the excitement and fear that went with it. That feeling is something to be remembered, cherished, and brought back to life. Otherwise, you'll lose what began as fun and as an intellectual challenge.

Below are a few simple techniques that can make your written communication alive again.

ENVISION YOUR READER

As you write each pleading, each brief, pretend that the reader is right there, right in front of you. Would he easily understand your point? Would she be nodding approval, or frowning in confusion?

My first suggestion is to *envision your audience*, your reader, as some person who will actually react to your written words—not someone who will move the bulk of pages into the right cubbyhole, but some individual who will read the words you write. I use this technique and I envision my grandmother, a farmer with a sixth-grade education; she was also suspicious of lawyers. My prose level, then, attempts to appease her while informing her, to make her feel comfortable with my advice and not feel defensive. In reality, an attorney's frequent reader is a law clerk or tired colleague, people who may not be suspicious but who are probably too busy to want to spend much time on yet another brief.

The very formats of legal writing are off-putting to those who aren't familiar with them; for those who are, the formats signal serious, dense information. Have you ever examined a contract, an agreement, a formulated pleading from a client's perspective, or from another tired attorney's perspective? Here are a few simple devices that open up documents and allow white space to enter those thick black blobs of ink that litter legal pages:

1. Leave margins.
2. Add subheads.
3. Enumerate items and indent the list.
4. Stick in graphics when possible.
5. Watch for overuse of underlining and capitalizing.

CONCENTRATE ON YOUR READERS' PRIORITIES

Thinking as if you were the audience, decide the most important element of the document for that clerk, that boss, that subordinate. *That's* the information that needs to go right up front. To get the information up front, where your reader wants it, experienced legal writers have to shift priorities; you have to approach your rough draft with the reader in mind and shift the original organization from your initial research path to your professional conclusion.

Here's a hypothetical example: your supervising attorney has asked you to review a draft version of a personnel policy document before it's sent out. As you read through it, you might make notes about each section or major idea. But how then would you organize those responses for the supervisor? Would you discuss them paragraph by paragraph? Would you interpret option by option? Thinking of your supervisor's priorities, you might instead give an introductory summary of your main points. You might say, for instance, that you agree with three of your supervisor's suggestions but find it hard to imagine that the proposed new policy on maternity leave doesn't break half the laws of the continental United States. Surely the supervisor knows which section of the ensuing discussion to read first.

If you're preparing a pleading or brief for the court, tell the judge what you want her to do, to whom, and why. Judges tell us that *good* writers introduce, in the first paragraph, the parties, the issue, and its intended resolution. When the initial information is not there, they get irritated. And since these are the judges who decide the case, irritating them may be counterproductive.

MAKE THE READING CLEAR

I should be able to read anything you write and at least follow the idea. I'm not a lawyer, not an expert in your field, but I'm an educated reader; your prose style should resemble the prose of other educated Americans. It should resemble American English. Characteristics of legal writing that separate it from mainstream writing should be edited out where possible.

A. Long sentences: The Company agrees to indemnify, defend, and hold harmless Buyer and all direct and indirect customers of Buyer with respect to any cost, legal expenses, damages, and injunctions arising from any claim of infringement by a third party against or arising from Buyer's use of the material, any such proprietary information and processes, or against or arising from Buyer's use of sale of the products produced in accordance with the practice of any said proprietary information and processes or by the use of such products by any direct or indirect customer of Buyer.

B. Separation of subject and verb: Similar restraints by a manufacturer to limit intrabrand competition in a situation where there was a heavy intrabrand competition were upheld in *Muenster Butane, Inc. v. Stewart Co.*, 651 F.2d 292 (5th Cir. 1981).

C. Jargon/repetitive language: In consideration of $10.00 cash in hand paid and other good and valuable considerations, the receipt and sufficiency of which we hereby acknowledge, Company hereby assigns, transfers, and conveys to Samuel Smith all of Company's title, interest, and rights in the inventions, discoveries, formulas, plans, files, notebooks, and records including, without limitation, all items associated with or in a commercial way used by Company.

D. Unnecessary passives: The funds were disbursed by Terri Miller at the closing by delivering a check to Savings and Loan. In addition, a check was paid to McDonald and another check was paid to the Insurance Company.

E. Unnecessary words that add to length: It is important to note that the earlier discussion of the computation of time periods is relevant here. . . . However, it must be noted that under one statutory interpretation, the ninety-day period is computed from the original due date.

   F. Obtrusive citations: Defendants contend that whether an allegedly fraudulent misrepresentation or omission was materially misleading must be determined in light of the "total mix" of information available to an investor, *TSE Industries, Inc. v. Northway, Inc.*, 426 U.S. 438, 449, 96 S. Ct. 2126, 2132, 48 L.Ed.2d 757 (1976); *Hassig v. Pearson*, 565 F.2d 644, 649-650, (10th Cir. 1977), and that materiality as derived from the "total mix" must be determined on a case-by-case basis according to the fact pattern of each specific transaction, *Radiation Dynamics, Inc. v. Goldmuntz*, 464 F.2d 876, 888 (2d Cir. 1972).

GET HELP

If you have just looked at the above examples and didn't see anything wrong with them, don't be ashamed to get help. If you wanted to be a litigator but couldn't get up in front of a group and *speak*, you'd hire a speech consultant to help you. (It's always curious to me how much attention attorneys pay to speaking, even though for many, their day-to-day jobs are mostly writing. Remember that your readers will judge your professionalism by your *writing*. Most of them will never hear you speak.)

   Here are some practical tips for additional help:

   1. If you aren't your own best editor, get *someone else* to edit your writing. Talk someone into the buddy system of exchange.

   2. Study to overcome your deficiencies. You don't have to sign up for a three-hour-a-week college class in technical writing—you don't have the time. But you could take a continuing legal education course, or you could arrange for a tutor.

   3. Another self-help aid is a contemporary reference book. You need both a new dictionary and a current grammar text.

   To summarize, let's review my suggestions for enlivening your legal prose by returning to my opening analogy.

   1. To put feeling back into your touch, fantasize. Familiarity can actually help you here: think of all the details of the person you're touching. Or, in legal writing, visualize your audience and make your document appeal to the reader.

2. Imagine what your "partner" wants. What are the priorities of that person as opposed to you? Sure, you've got a lot to offer, but feeling comes back into touch when you know you're pleasing the other person. Or, in legal writing, be up front. Tell readers what they want to know in a concise, up-front, and organized manner.

3. Present an attractive package your partner can't turn down. No one wants to touch someone who's unattractive. You can make the package attractive by exercising away all that unnecessary fat. Or, in legal writing, make your prose readable.

4. Finally, if you've forgotten or never learned the proper technique for touching, it's not too late to learn. There are all kinds of books on the subject, as well as willing tutors. And the same is true for legal experts who want to produce expert prose. (See Chapter 30 for recommended materials.)

*Query: Which profession had to invent an 8½ × 14"
sheet of paper? Not physicians—they have always
managed with notepads. Even serious scholars have
accepted the restraints of an 8½ × 11" sheet.*

(Note: Contemporary federal courts require 8½ × 11" or smaller
[6⅛ × 9¼"]. Patent courts still allow a variety of page sizes for blueprints
and so on.)

3

FOCUS ON DENSITY

Readers' eyes glaze over as they skim a single-spaced, legal-sized document for three pages, waiting to find the end of the first paragraph—one that begins with "Whereas" and ends with a semicolon. The next paragraphs begin the same way; after countless pages, readers find the elusive "Therefore be it resolved that . . ." or "Therefore it is agreed that . . ." and the last paragraph rambles to a conclusion. The careful, precise legal expert can say that she has written a referential document, not an informative one; that the material is meant to cover the legal contingencies, not to be read by the many parties involved. But at best, readers correctly consider legal writing "dense," that is, difficult to read. No reader can keep the contents of a three-page paragraph in mind.

Although legal writing is frequently dense, its format, the visual impression, doesn't have to match its density. Legal writers might add some balancing white space; they can create the appearance of a less-dense document by manipulating margins, paragraph length, and line spacing; they can also incorporate the stylistic devices of enumeration, tabulation, headings, and subheadings.

GENEROUS MARGINS

Adding white space changes the page's visual impact. Generous margins give the eyes a rest and can subtly suggest that an expert writer cares about the reader, that she wants to paint a balanced picture instead of smearing black ink across the page.

DOUBLE-SPACING

Another simple technique for adding white space is to double-space. In-house documents are hard to read; the single-spaced lines melt together and they're uninviting. It's as if writers don't believe they need to make in-house material appealing even though the majority of their reading is itself produced within the firm or agency. Legal writers show more respect for their judicial audience by double-spacing except for direct quotes.

FORMAL TABULATIONS

White space is also the product of formal tabulation, a listing of grammatically parallel items that follow either no punctuation or a colon. Notice the open space around the two examples below. The items tabulated must belong to the same class and be parallel in structure, with a common idea introduced before the tabulation. If each tabulated item makes up an integral part of the introductory sentence, no punctuation is needed before the list. Writers should remember

1. to indent all of each item and to number each item;
2. to begin each item with a lowercase letter;
3. to end each item except the last with a comma or a semicolon;
4. to use a comma or semicolon and *and* or *or* on the next-to-last item; and
5. to conclude the last item with a period *unless* the list does not conclude the sentence.

Experienced writers can also use formal tabulation to organize simple lists and set them apart from the rest of the blocked text. If they choose to add white space through the list form of tabulation, writers should check for six provisions:

1. Colon introduction.
2. Indentation.
3. Grammatical parallel.
4. Capital letters.
5. Periods at end.
6. No *and* or *or*.

Not only do these two methods help the reader understand the connection between the introduction and its subsequent parts, but the white space around the tabulation separates it from the rest of the text. Thus, if writers want to emphasize errors in their opponent's briefs, tabulating will highlight them—all that white space entices the eye. Tabulation can also help summarize important material. Here, for instance, the introduction to a lease uses only a few lines; the complete lease can be attached at the end of the accompanying letter or memorandum, if necessary, and not intrude on the reader's ability to read the memorandum.

```
The following sections of the lease, summarized
here, are relevant to this case:
    2.4 States an explicit covenant of quiet enjoy-
        ment.
    3.2 Prohibits activities offensive to other ten-
        ants or their patrons.
    3.3 Prohibits material changes in commercial
        property without the owner's consent.
    9.3 Gives the landlord the unrestricted right to
        evict a tenant for breach of any covenant.
```

ENUMERATIONS WITHIN SENTENCES

If the list isn't important enough to highlight as shown above, writers can still enumerate within sentences, using semicolons and commas to signal parallel items following the introductory statement. Although the result isn't as emphatic, because the text doesn't receive added white space, the reader has been cued to the sentence's hierarchy with punctuation that gives a sense of closure even if the items are not numbered. Enumerating within a sentence also takes less space.

```
A family member may donate organs for several
traditional reasons: helping others for the com-
mon good (altruism), mitigating the death of the
family member so that something good will come of
the relative's death, providing a memorial for the
deceased, fulfilling the deceased relative's in-
tention to donate, or taking advantage of the op-
portunity to rehabilitate the deceased's reputa-
tion by a final positive act.
```

Notice that both tabulation and enumeration require grammatically parallel items and consistent punctuation.

INFORMAL TABULATIONS

Within an informal document (office memorandum, announcement), writers may use informal tabulation, a listing that follows asterisks (*), bullet dots, or dashes (typed as two hyphens). Informal tabulation creates white space while allowing writers the freedom to jot down grammatically unrelated material.

```
The annual practice of hiring summer clerks has
overextended our budget:
• clerks—$600-800 a week
• many clerks never complete an assignment within
  their six-week stay
• the entertainment budget for 12 clerks would have
  paid the salary of a full-time associate for the
  next year
• travel and housing-adjustment pay
  Would you please consider each of these expenses
  and be prepared by the Monday meeting to suggest
  ways to get this budget back into reality? I know
  we want to be competitive. But . . .
```

Naturally, content would dictate the practicality of informal tabulation.

HEADINGS AND SUBHEADINGS

A final suggestion for adding white space to enhance readability is the use of headings and subheadings. Experienced litigators already know the value of headings; they emphasize the major points and counterpoints of the argument. By their placement, their capital letters and underlining, and the white space around them, they yell for the reader's attention. If headings can help briefs, they should also greatly improve memoranda.

■■■

Because attorneys read memoranda more frequently than briefs, writers should remember their daily audience and add liberal white space to enhance readability.

> *The creative process is as individualistic as legal writers themselves. Solutions to writer's block can't be prescriptive but must be adjusted to each writer.*

4
ATTORNEYS AND WRITER'S BLOCK

I have never heard a practicing attorney admit to problems with writer's block. As a consultant and editor, I see only the final product and do not get to observe the total writing process. The other day, however, I walked among a group of high school students preparing for a University Interscholastic League (UIL) Ready-Writing contest. These high school juniors and seniors were geared up, primed to compete against each other in the statewide competition. Ten minutes after we gave them the topic, some were still gazing into space. Twenty minutes later, a few were doodling on scratch sheets, obvious victims of writer's block. Their contest is timed; these hapless few were frozen, waiting for that flash of inspiration that would make them competitive. It was only as I worried about their anguished faces that I realized that I do not get to see such suffering among attorneys. Do attorneys have the same problem?

Writer's block is usually associated with creative writing (novels, poems, cartoons, personal opinion columns in magazines and newspapers) and with on-the-spot writing (tests, in-class essays, and competitive writing such as the UIL contest that initiated this question). Interestingly, I have heard attorneys argue that legal writing is not intended to be creative, that it is instead a logical exercise that develops through research from question to issue to conclusion, and to them creativity is either unnecessary or a frill. If that is true, then attorneys for some utilitarian reasons might not ever suffer writer's block:

1. They cannot afford writer's block. A client's bill is supposed to relate to the task performed. Few clients would consider it reasonable to pay by the hour while an attorney waits for those creative sparks to ignite the beginning of a letter or memorandum or contract.

2. Deadlines do not leave time for writer's block. Practicing attorneys are controlled by deadlines, and procrastination results not in a late product but in a hastily thrown-together one that meets a deadline.

3. They work from a question toward an answer and can depend on research to lead them. Unlike school assignments or ready-writing contests, legal documents are frequently designed around a predictable research path, one that will be followed by both plaintiff and defendant, for instance, or by attorneys supporting state lawmakers as well as attorneys representing taxpayers fighting a specific application of that law. Thus, the skeleton of a legal document is frequently, though not always, preordained by existing law.

"Fair enough," a reader might respond, "but what about those days when I really cannot find any cases on point, or I have so much research material that I cannot dive right in and make sense of it? That might not conform to a technical definition of writer's block, but I am stumped and cannot begin. At those times I have just as much trouble beginning to write as anyone else, and the pressure of a deadline makes it more nerve-racking than an in-class paper."

I can suggest a number of techniques for overcoming writer's block, all the while recognizing that the creative process is just as individualistic as legal writers themselves. Thus, a discussion of this sort is limited to a description of, rather than prescription for, methods of prewriting and organization that seem to work for other writers.

NOTHING TO SAY

Not having anything to say is the more difficult of our responder's two problems; if she cannot find anything in the books after her initial research, she still has to commit something to paper, usually before she can leave the office, no matter how late. One technique for solving her problem is a return to the classic devices for "invention," that is, the methods to spur the creative process. Perhaps the most familiar of these is the tree diagram, in which a writer begins with a central word or phrase and divides the initial "tree trunk" idea into branches to help get ideas for writing (see Figure 1). Using a tree diagram, a writer would first consider each aspect of the client's fact situation. Each major issue

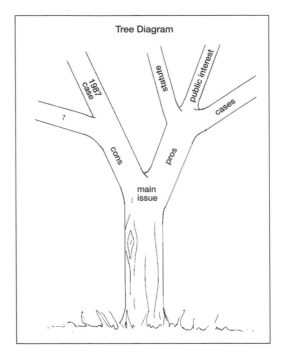

Figure 1

becomes the basis of a trunk, the issues written perhaps on separate sheets of paper to allow free doodling. From each central word or phrase, the writer divides the issue into two or more subissues, branches of the tree. If both are viable options, both are then explored. If one proves to be a dead end, the remaining branch is again divided until the writer is satisfied.

Many of us have used tree diagramming; Gabriele Lusser Rico's *Writing the Natural Way*[1] expands the concept with the introduction of "clustering," in which a central word spawns associations (see Figure 2). For the process to work, writers have to be willing to let go of rigid patterns of thought and allow all possible associations to emerge—encouraging serendipity, which is discovering something valuable when it was not even particularly sought. If the writer can scribble the little bubbles of thought without an internal censor limiting the process, the result can be a full page of words and cases and terms and perhaps even metaphors that the more rational mind can sort through later. The important point

---

[1] Gabriele Lusser Rico, Writing the Natural Way 28–48 (1983).

for attorneys to realize is that not everything listed in a tree diagram or cluster has to be used in the final creation of the document or argument; much will seem at first outside the boundaries of the question, and indeed, some will prove to be. But who is to say that a childhood memory of "roller skates" in reference to the initial term *trespass* cannot provoke another set of images that may lead the writer to a novel solution?

A third method of generating ideas is "cubing." It can work in tandem with or separately from the above devices and goes like this: suppose the writer has a tree diagram or a cluster of information and still does not know what to do with the issue. She can generate ideas by formulating a variety of searching questions that help the research by guiding her response to specific questions. This device, obviously, provides slightly more structure for the creative search. The writer can draw a cube and label each side with a leading question. The questions may be the result of earlier tree diagramming or clustering, or she may intuitively know the questions but need impetus or specific paths for finding an answer. Obvious general questions can initiate a stream of written responses: Why? What? How? When? Where? Who is a good source? Is

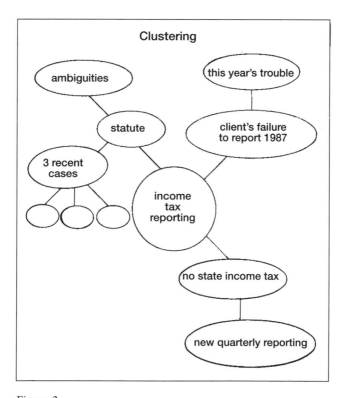

Figure 2

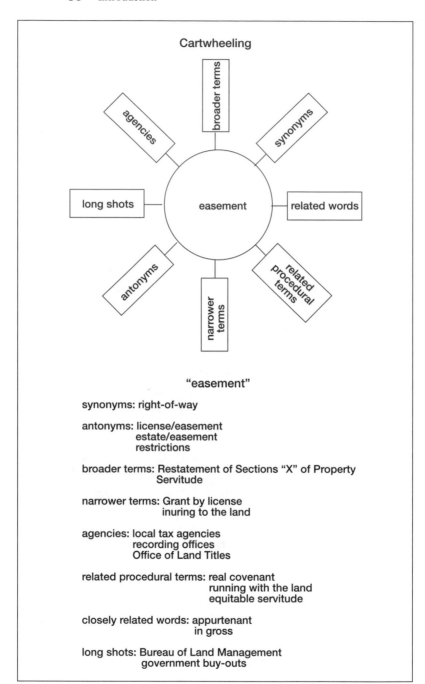

Cartwheeling

broader terms

agencies

synonyms

long shots — easement — related words

antonyms

narrower terms

related procedural terms

"easement"

synonyms: right-of-way

antonyms: license/easement
estate/easement
restrictions

broader terms: Restatement of Sections "X" of Property
Servitude

narrower terms: Grant by license
inuring to the land

agencies: local tax agencies
recording offices
Office of Land Titles

related procedural terms: real covenant
running with the land
equitable servitude

closely related words: appurtenant
in gross

long shots: Bureau of Land Management
government buy-outs

Figure 3

this issue like anything I have ever seen before? Have these clients ever needed help before? What would my law professor suggest I do here? What position will the opposing side take? If the writer separates answers into columns or uses separate sheets of paper for each major prompting question, she can mull over the results and find different combinations that may spur the inquiry into a new direction. The object of the experiment is to accumulate data, connections. If this prewriting experience works, writers will have some strategy already committed to paper; they may even have some organizational options in front of them.

Making the term *invention* specifically relevant to legal researchers, William Statsky suggests the "cartwheel,"[2] which can produce key terms for researchers who have not initially found relevant (or any) cases (see Figure 3). Instead of the free-form associations of tree diagramming and clustering, Statsky suggests legal writers begin with a troublesome broad term ("easement") and create lists of words and phrases around this term: synonyms, antonyms, broader terms, narrower terms, agencies that deal with the area, related procedural terms, closely related words, and long shots. With the resulting list, researchers can again explore the indexes and tables of contents of law books.

TOO MUCH MATERIAL

The second problem our hypothetical writer might encounter is an abundance of material. Each question may turn up four or five options, each with its own subcategories of possibilities. How can a writer pull the resulting disparate material together? Similarly, every path may lead to a quagmire of even more legal issues that themselves lead to a plethora of cases. Overload can produce writer's block, which can again stop the writing process. Legal writers cannot afford to read and summarize every case that Shepardizing turns up. Faced with this mountain of information, many writers simply stop because the volume overcomes their abilities to set priorities and establish a realistic outline. Unfortunately, establishing priorities is easier at the conclusion of research than at the beginning, because you learn along the way to distinguish some material from other material.

So what can you do if everything in the law library seems to pertain to your case, if your office is covered with open books or printouts and thirty points that all sound relevant? A useful start is to stand back from the material and determine if there is one issue the case will

---

[2] William Statsky, Torts: Personal Injury Litigation 19–22 (1982).

stand or fall on. If so, then of course you must concentrate on it. If not, decide what larger issue encompasses several of the others. If you can articulate that concept, then you can list elements essential for the major argument. If you have two major concerns, these items should be coordinated, made equal in both placement and support. The other issues may fit into the major issue as subissues. If not, they should probably be discarded so you can focus your efforts.

Even after writers decide on their major issue, writer's block can still stymie them. They can try, of course, to weed out irrelevant cases and obscure statutes for a start. Discarding the old and out-of-state cases and those with wildly different fact situations can reduce the clutter and allow the creative process to advance. Here, unfortunately, many otherwise strong writers falter and retain all the cases they have uncovered just to ensure that they do not omit an important point. Other writers include the extraneous material because it takes too much time to sift through the stack. It is easier for them to write around the entirety and reach the conclusion in a hurry than it is to stop the process and develop an organizational scheme that makes the best use of the best authority.

ORGANIZING AROUND WRITER'S BLOCK

Once writers narrow their field of material, the next problem that can overcome a writer is organization. Many writers have found that experimenting with a provisional organizing principle can yield results. That is, they choose one organizational pattern and allow it to function as an impetus for sifting through the remaining ideas. They look for an organization that creates an airtight letter, argument, or discussion. They question alternative organizational patterns that achieve a more successful result. Experimenting with one pattern and then another helps the writer understand more about the argument and thus judge which aspect of the discussion is the strongest. The final organizational patterns should emphasize the major idea and relegate the rest to subordinate positions.

To be able to choose from several possibilities, writers might scribble two or three quick rough drafts in the same time it would normally take to write one good semifinished draft. These rough drafts may be wild stabs in the dark, wanderings, and irrelevant rabbit trails. But if writers limit their time to fifteen or twenty minutes for each wild stab, keep a list of statutes and cases before them, and allow their ideas some latitude, they may discover the issue will begin to make sense. This phase may be the one bona fide excuse for a dictating machine; you can speak in a conversational voice, talking to yourself or an imaginary cohort, and chat about two or three ways of explaining the problem. Thought does not become concrete until it is articulated or written, so this conversational phase may allow you to see what you did not even know you wanted to say.

As you read your rough drafts or transcripts of the dictation, underline or star the ideas you want to keep and concentrate on organizing them so that they complete your purpose (inform, argue, both) for your audience. Writers who expect the first draft to become the final product expect too much of themselves and probably thus encourage writer's block in the draft stage. Finally, when you have begun to feel comfortable with the content you have developed, you can shift gears to the editing stage, where you can revise and tinker with your draft.

EDITING BELONGS IN THE FINAL STAGE

Nit-picking each word and idea as you write defeats the purpose of writing drafts. No writer can envision the larger organizational pattern and conclusion and simultaneously worry about dangling participles. Editing neurosis stills the pen not only of weak writers who are anticipating errors but also of excellent writers who worry themselves to a standstill thinking every draft should represent a polished document. Only after the draft is written should the legal writer shift jobs from being a creator to being an editor and proofreader. Hold off editing: the creative process can be blocked at any stage if writers shift concentration from the larger picture to the stylistic details.

5

MIN(D)ING THE FIELD
Appellate Judges Speak Out

A frequent audience of legal writing is the judiciary, so I asked twenty-five judges on the Texas courts of appeals about their responses to legal writing. Their answers provide a glimpse of the sequestered mental process of the men and women on the bench. I was curious about their answers because attorneys insist that the courts require them to conform to a traditional, formulated style. The judges' responses satisfied my curiosity. They may also help writers who have never separated the people who read briefs from the institutional aura of the court.

RECORD REFERENCES

The most frequent complaint of appellate judges is the omission of record references. When judges read opposing briefs, record references help them turn to the trial record or exhibits for clarification. Therefore, attorneys writing for these courts can provide easy access to the record by first understanding which testimony and exhibits the judges want to review. These appellate judges were not at the trial, did not hear the testimony, and have not met the parties. Experienced appellate writers have learned to substantiate the backgrounds of their clients and the case so that the judge or clerk does not have to review the entire transcript looking for backup information.

POINTS OF ERROR

Second on the judges' list of pet peeves: too many points of error. Seven to ten points within any brief was the maximum number for the judges.

They are dismayed by points that are repeated in slightly different language and by writers who do not condense the points into coherent groups. Judges become confused when the writers do not "identify the *real* point requiring reversal." And they complain, understandably, that briefs are burdened (and therefore the judges are burdened) with "throw-away" points of error, or points so muddled that they cannot understand what the problem is and what relief is sought.

Obviously, attorneys are concerned about points of error—they do not want to be charged with failing to raise legitimate issues. One solution you might consider would be outlining major points and grouping together those of a similar nature under a generalized heading. Instead of listing six different errors within the statement of facts as six separate errors, for example, perhaps you can group them as one error. You can discuss and document each error separately, within one section, even though several errors fall within the same major heading. Be careful, of course, not to confuse the judge and therefore forfeit an argument by burying a point under an illogical heading.

CITATIONS

Citations create the third reading block for the judges. They expressed anger over citations that do not support the principle or holding being discussed. They also become confused when the writer fails to indicate what a cited case stands for. And like other legal readers, appellate judges dislike string citations because they add bulk, but not law, to briefs. One judge wrote that he especially abhorred excessive citations in lieu of reasoning, because the writer was expecting the judge to do the work. He feels, understandably, that getting through the two briefs and supplemental materials is already enough work.

Perhaps the gravest error an appellate writer can commit is to misstate a citation, for once judges discover discrepancies—caused by whatever reason—they are inevitably forced to question the authenticity of the entire brief. Although the judges did not estimate the percent of the briefs that contain inaccurate citations, five judges listed it as the major problem.

OPPONENT'S POINTS

A final major problem for several judges is the failure of the appellant's brief to respond to the appellee's principal arguments and authorities. Brief writers need to respond to all key arguments or positions of the opponents. If the judges read the opposing briefs simultaneously, balancing points and arguments, they must draw the conclusion that one side cannot counter the other's argument if it is not mentioned or is insufficiently documented.

Perhaps brief writers, failing to address their opponent's points, are hoping that their own arguments are so convincing that the court will overlook the opposition's points. Neither judges nor I would recommend that strategy.

FOOTNOTES

All but one of the judges approve of footnotes for nonessential material. However, few find it easy to read sentences with footnotes located in the middle; it makes sense, then, to organize the sentence so that the footnote, indicating a record reference or point elaboration, falls at the end of the sentence. Example: "If Marvelous Marvin proves either one of those causes of action, he will be entitled to appropriate damages, but several defenses in this case should prevent him from recovery."[1] [[1]Appellee has prepared a flow chart attached as Exhibit A to help explain the defenses to the two causes of action that are applicable under the facts of this case.]

Not one of the judges approves of sentences with more than one footnote. But they are evenly divided about placing long citations at the bottom of the page as a footnote. To summarize, use footnotes when you think they are necessary, but do so as unobtrusively as possible.

HEADINGS AND SUBHEADINGS

Headings and subheadings make briefs more readable by emphasizing major points and their relationship to each other. As an experiment, you might read a brief with all the headings removed—I doubt you could follow the logic in even your own brief.

Most judges accept incomplete sentences for headings and subheadings (*"III. Duty to Warn"*) because they are concise and to the point. Complete sentences, especially in subheadings, create unnecessary words. But half of the judges disapprove of stacking headings and subheadings because it creates choppy reading. Try this example:

```
I. Real Estate Broker/Principal Relationship
   A. Relationship
      1. "Middleman" Distinguished
```

If your discussion within any section is short enough, you will not need subheadings—they're necessary only when several elements make up one point you are emphasizing.

QUOTATIONS

All but two judges expect quotations longer than fifty words to be blocked and single-spaced. Harvard's *Bluebook* (*A Uniform System of Citation*) also sets this limit. But I might add a word of caution: long quotations are easy to skim or simply skip. If an outside authority can advance your argument in language more convincing than your own, quote it. But first introduce the source and essential meaning of the quotation in your tag line; that is, summarize what readers are to expect, or at least entice them into the quotation with a carefully worded introductory phrase. Then if the reader's eye slips past the blocked material, you have at least introduced that important idea—not buried it within a block of black print.

Incorporating two or more quotations in the same sentence, with a separate footnote for each, appeals to only a few judges. Multiple quotations succeed only when several authorities make parallel points and the sentences ring with clarity, despite quotation marks and little subscript numbers. But only three judges could muster "no opinion" about the multiple quotations; everyone else disapproved.

Finally, in a paragraph containing a quotation, you will help the reader by discussing the relevant law or theory first. That way your reader has a context for your material. If a quotation introduces an idea or section, readers skim through it to reach the point—and perhaps miss its significance.

▬▬▬

Appellate judges admitted they spend an average of sixteen hours a week writing their own opinions; they average twenty-one hours a week reading briefs before they begin writing. That emphasis on reading and writing makes them particularly sensitive to words, sentences, phrases, and organization of long briefs. An overwhelming majority of the judges, when asked what part of the appellate process they rely on most—the brief, oral argument, or a clerk's summary of the briefs and memoranda—chose written briefs. Reading briefs allows them an opportunity to double-check authorities; because the words are frozen, the judges can refer back to them when they begin to synthesize the steps behind their final opinions. If members of the court have an easier time reading briefs, they will have more time to consider each case. They will also have time to read more briefs.

All readers—whether of fiction, poetry, journalism, or legal writing—enjoy clear and concise writing. And, characteristically human, judges are bound to be affected by the style of the brief writer.

II
MANIPULATING
LEGAL SENTENCES
First Aid

6

THE LONG SENTENCE

David Mellinkoff is not asking that legal writers ignore significant facts or omit sections of argument; he is, however, reminding writers that the more legal experience they have, the greater their tendency to display all of their knowledge in one sentence.

His advice goes for the most part unheeded. Law offices are stacked with overflowing file cabinets. Ceiling-to-floor boxes of documents stifle courthouses. Nevertheless, legal writers scribble and type away, adding sentence after sentence to page after page, ream after ream of paper. The longer they practice law, the more stock phrases they know and the more contingencies they realize have to be covered for each idea.

The sentence as a unit is manageable, or should be. Even long sentences can work—from a legal perspective. But they don't work rhetorically, and they thus cause readers time and headaches. Following Mellinkoff's advice, we will investigate ways to cover the subject and admit to necessary contingencies, and yet to either say less or put a period in the middle.

SAY LESS

When writers economize and choose their words carefully, they can actually say more—but in less space. But it is an uphill battle against difficult options, competing precedent, and daily time pressures. We rarely focus on techniques for getting that point across. On the theory that recognizing flabby writing helps you trim your own, let us look at a sample sentence.

```
Defendant made a motion for summary judgment and
the court granted the defendant's motion holding
that parol evidence was inadmissible to vary the
terms of the written agreement and that the con-
tract was one for an indefinite term and was there-
fore terminable at will by the defendant employer.
```

Perhaps the author could excise this flabby demon by *eliminating the obviously unnecessary words*. Why explain in a separate sentence that the defendant had made the motion for summary judgment? The writer can eliminate seven unnecessary words by simply combining two ideas into a single phrase:

```
The court granted First Bank's motion for summary
judgment.
```

The added touch of switching "Defendant" to "First Bank" helps the judge follow the narrative along without flipping back to remember who's who. The second holding of the court needs to be separated into a new sentence: "The court also held. . . ."

Many compound constructions can be replaced with a single word and are easy to spot if you practice day-to-day editing. It is difficult to recognize these unnecessary words in your own writing, but this list may serve as a reminder:

```
at this point in time (now)
went on to say (said)
inasmuch as (since)
for the reason that (because)
in the event that (if)
in order to (to)
prior to (before)
subsequent to (after)
with a view to (to)
```

The following expressions are rarely necessary:

```
it should be pointed out that
the question as to whether
```

```
there is/there are
it is a fact that
clearly
```

A second step toward reducing monster sentences is to *eliminate repetitions*. Repetitions, or redundancies, end up in documents because these phrases are so familiar that writers do not question them:

```
lease agreement
false misrepresentation
past history
mutual agreement
```

When legal writers add to these common redundancies the specialized legal ones, they produce dense, unintelligible prose:

```
alter or change
cease and desist
force and effect
free and clear
null and void
order and direct
save and except
unless and until
```

A third technique for "saying less" is to *eliminate unnecessary
jargon* (see Chapter 18). Now, most lawyers hear complaints about
legal jargon from everyone—from their mothers, dentists, and casual
passersby. The problem of jargon, therefore, is not a surprise, but it may
be surprising to recognize how long a sentence becomes when it is burdened with unnecessary jargon:

```
enclosed herewith
said funds were given
shall henceforth be called
the aforesaid party
hereinafter referred to as
```

How can legal writers say less if they continue to lean on these comfortable phrases that add nothing but bulk? Our example above contains
some necessary legal expressions: "summary judgment," "parol evidence," and "terminable at will." They are terms of art that need to

remain in the sentence unless it is altered for a layperson. The terms of art are shorthand for concepts the intended audience—judges and clerks—will know. To explain each of these concepts would not only add unnecessary words to the sentence but would also confuse or insult the intended reader.

Below are flabby sentences you can edit for practice.

```
1. Prior to the trial, she consulted with her attor-
   ney in regard to her inheritance.
2. Inasmuch as she asked, he insisted she return the
   retainer for the purpose of taxes.
3. There is no other method, except in trial, in
   which Mr. Corley can obtain this material.
4. The mutual agreement will be null and void unless
   and until Mr. Corley decides to order and direct
   his legal representatives to alter or change the
   offending paragraphs.
```

PUT A PERIOD IN THE MIDDLE

Mellinkoff's second suggestion, taken to absurdity, would produce sentence fragments with tiny jolts of information. But if the period symbolizes closure, then effective writers following this advice would limit sentences to only one idea and would punctuate longer clauses with appropriate closure marks (sets of commas, periods, semicolons, parentheses, colons) that allow the reader's eye to pause.

If your sentences average more than twenty-five words, or if they average longer than four typed lines, consider making them more accessible to the readers by providing closure. Long is not wrong, but long is more difficult to understand and retain. Legal concepts are frequently already difficult enough to follow without the added complexity of a ten-line sentence. Obviously, of course, not all sentences need to contain twenty-five words either—that would create monotony and probably some strange results. What experienced writers strive toward is prose that can be read and understood the first time through because each sentence contains only one idea or has punctuation that allows independent ideas to flow logically.

Cut a long sentence into two or more sentences if the result is acceptable. Look at our example when it is divided into two separate sentences:

```
The court granted First City's motion for summary
judgment. The court also held that parol evidence
```

```
was inadmissible to vary the terms of the written
agreement, that the contract was one for an indefi-
nite term, and that the contract was terminable at
will by the employer.
```

Putting a period in the middle separates the court's holdings from its procedural decision and emphasizes the distinction.

An alternative to a period is a *semicolon*, which functions as both a period and a transition. Semicolons allow sophisticated writers to separate main ideas into sentences yet signal to the reader the close relationship between the ideas.

```
The court granted First City's motion for summary
judgment; the court also held that parol evidence
was inadmissible to vary the terms of the written
agreement, that the contract was one for an indefi-
nite term, and that the contract was terminable at
will by the employer.
```

A third punctuation device to help long sentences is to *number* and list elements within a sentence (to *tabulate*), carefully and systematically organizing parallel sentence elements. Legal writers do not take advantage of this option as much as they could; tabulation helps both the writer to organize and the reader to follow lengthy recitations. Either of the following methods helps organize the material and make it more accessible for the reader:

```
The court granted First City's motion for summary
judgment; the court also held (1) that parol evi-
dence was inadmissible to vary the terms of the
written agreement, (2) that the contract was one
for an indefinite term, and (3) that the contract
was terminable at will by the employer.
```

```
The court granted First City's motion for summary
judgment; the court also held:
     1. that parol evidence was inadmissible to vary
        the terms of the written agreement,
     2. that the contract was one for an indefinite
        term, and
     3. that the contract was terminable at will by
        the employer.
```

Working under the theory that practicing careful writing creates careful writers, I have included the following sentences, taken from a legal journal, for your practice. Can you find a logical place to add a period? commas? tabulation?

1. In an attempt to mitigate the harshness of this doctrine, the courts developed the idea of constructive eviction whereby a tenant could assert that the condition of the premises was such that they were unlivable and therefore he had been "constructively evicted" by his landlord.

2. If we endeavor to find within legal education a conception of successful legal education, and hence the prevailing conception of the good lawyer, a dominant, quite familiar answer is there: Legal education, when it is done successfully and well, will produce graduates who will be good lawyers, technically proficient in, at, and with the law—persons who understand how to engage in legal analysis and the construction and assessment of legal argument, who understand and can employ adeptly and imaginatively legal doctrines and concepts, and who can and will bring skills and knowledge of this sort regularly and fully to bear upon any matter of concern to any client willing and able to employ them in order to further the client's interest, provided only that they, as lawyers, do not do what the law prohibits lawyers from doing for clients.

CONCLUSION

Especially in literature, long sentences create a rhythm that enhances the separate words' meanings. William Faulkner needed complex sentence structure to entangle readers with the facets of his characters. Ken Kesey needed rambling paragraphs to emphasize the parallels between generations in *Sometimes a Great Notion*. Unfortunately, long sentences do not work as well for lawyers, perhaps because lawyers' messages are usually technical and embedded in precedent. In literature, the final ambiance, the attitudes, the images left in the readers' minds are paramount. Typical fiction readers do not inspect novels and short stories for the dangling character, the elliptical fragment, or ambiguous definitions.

Legal writing, in contrast, is studied, evaluated, and picked apart word by word, phrase by phrase. Even when legal writers tell a story (e.g., in the statement of facts), the effect of that story depends on accuracy, on believability, on the reader's clear understanding of the minute elements in the story. The legal story depends on sentence structure to hold it together and provide its skeletal structure. If the skeleton is so embedded in flab that the reader cannot discern the structure over and around it, then the legal writer–storyteller has failed, no matter how serious or well researched the facts.

Ever have that tired, low-down feeling before you finish reading a sentence? A major cause of sentence fatigue is the left-handed sentence, one that begins with a long series of dependent clauses that keeps readers waiting for the central subject.

7

LEFT-HANDED SENTENCES

Left-handed sentences place the burden of unraveling meaning on the readers; they must first read through and file away all the qualifiers before they locate and absorb the main subject and verb. After the belated discovery of the main idea, the readers then have to backtrack and apply the qualifiers to relevant nouns and verbs.

```
Given the treatment of computer software as tan-
gible personal property, the legislative elimina-
tion of the canned/custom software distinction,
expansion of the sales tax base to include data
processing services (effective Jan. 1, 1988), and
the definition of sale/purchase to include ser-
vices, the relevancy of this doctrine to computer
property and services in Texas has diminished
considerably.
```

Not all sentences that begin with dependent clauses create trouble with comprehension, of course. The sophisticated writer varies sentence structure, avoiding a constant subject-verb-object pattern, and uses beginning adverbial clauses appropriately (or sparingly). Properly constructed and controlled introductory clauses deliver variety and punch; they add to, rather than detract from, readability.

Let us look at a second example: how many qualifiers must you hold in abeyance before you reach the end of this next sentence (or the end of your patience)?

```
In order to achieve the highest degree of cer-
tainty that the transaction will not be voided
at a later time by a complaint that it is merely
a device by which to exact a usurious rate of
interest from the seller of the accounts (the
"seller"), it would be advisable to specify in the
purchase documents that there shall be no recourse
to the seller in the event that any of the ac-
counts should become uncollectible.
```

The first forty-six words keep us hanging. By the time we get to the last thirty, we are pretty unhappy readers, *if* we are reading at all. Separated out, the embedded clauses in the introduction contain several interdependent ideas:

```
• to achieve the highest degree of certainty
• certainty that the transaction will not be voided
• voided at a later time
• voided by a complaint
• a complaint that it is merely a device
• a device to exact a usurious rate of interest
```

Now, embedding per se does not create the problem in the sentence above; rather, the total weight of the string of embedded ideas together with its awkward placement creates a reading problem. Writers who create sentences like these are concentrating on the substance, on what they believe the readers need to *know*, rather than on what the reader can reasonably *understand.*

A legal writer in control of legal substance can concentrate on revising a draft sentence so that readers can more easily grasp its point. The simplest solution for a left-handed sentence is to flip-flop it until the main ideas, represented by the subject and verb, precede the subordinate qualifiers. A flip-flopping of the sentence above would allow readers to see the logical unfolding of the hierarchy of the parts (independent clauses and their subordinate modifiers) before reaching the forty-seventh word:

```
It would be advisable to specify in the purchase
documents that there shall be no recourse to the
seller of the accounts ("seller") in the event
that any of the accounts should become uncollect-
ible in order to achieve the highest degree of
certainty that the transaction will not be voided
```

```
at a later time by a complaint that it is merely a
device by which to exact a usurious rate of inter-
est from the seller.
```

Now the information in the sentence is accessible (even if it is still too long and dense). Those clauses explain *why* the documents need to be specific: they thus function as adverbs that can be moved after the verb, toward the end of the sentence.

A second cure for left-handed sentences is to break the introductory clauses into a separate sentence. Obviously our seventy-six-word sentence will benefit from such a division. We might even go so far as to delete a few words from the resulting two sentences:

```
We should specify in the purchase documents that
there shall be no recourse to the seller of the
accounts ("seller") if any of the accounts become
uncollectible; that way we can be sure that the
transaction will not be voided later by a com-
plaint that it is merely an artificial device for
exacting a usurious rate of interest from the
seller.
```

The resulting sixty-one words divided between two sentences are more manageable than the original. Additional tinkering with the new sentences would undoubtedly improve them even more, but at least we have moved the priority (the action) to the front and the subordinate (the justification for the action) to a position of less importance. Because of this change, readers can concentrate on the message instead of the sentence structure.

After you have written a rough draft and covered the substantive requirements of your document, you can return and reread it, sentence by sentence, from the perspective of your uninitiated readers—not unintelligent or uninterested, but readers who do not have a clue about where your next sentence will take them. You can shift your writing priority from the legal substance to the communication of it.

Dragging readers through unnecessary pages of superfluous words shall be a crime, just like filling a "real chocolate" Easter egg with gummy marshmallow.

8

MARSHMALLOW CONSTRUCTIONS

Pretentious prose is replete with "marshmallows": soft and pudgy sentences clogged with sugar and filler that add only air to the sentence. Careful editors can contract marshmallows to lean and mean sentences that carry punch, characterized by strong action verbs and lean, concrete nouns.

THE WINDUP

Marshmallow sentences wander sideways into the main point. Like watching a crab, viewers have a hard time anticipating direction or goal. A typical marshmallow sentence begins with a windup before the main punch. The windups bog down the central idea similar to a public speaker's "uh, well . . . ." Both initial hesitancies allow the author/speaker an opportunity to get thoughts together, but they annoy the reader/listener. They eventually create problems for the writer, too, because windups have a nasty habit of taking over prose; they become familiar crutches and thus show up repeatedly. If you are curious whether you wind up before you throw the punch, look through your writing for these marshmallow beginnings. Most of the bracketed words can be deleted; a few need only a single-word replacement:

```
[There is no question that] the police had no
prior information on the driver.
```

```
[The kind of] issue in these circumstances is
probable cause.
    [What we are concerned with] is the weight of
authority that a police officer's self-protective
search for weapons is justified.
    [The fact that] the police had no information
about the driver or circumstance does not warrant
a belief that the driver had committed a crime.
    [Owing to a] [Due to the fact that there is]
lack of evidence, the driver should not have had
his car searched.
    [In a short period of time] the driver produced
his license and insurance.
    [There are] several leading cases [that] help
resolve the issues presented in this case.
    [It is also apparent that] the driver made no
furtive gestures.
    [In order to] search the car, the police need
probable cause.
    [We must ascertain as to whether] facts and cir-
cumstances within the officer's knowledge at the
time of the initial stop warranted a belief that
the driver had committed a crime.
    [It is clear that] the requirement of probable
cause before a warrantless search is valid.
```

ABSTRACT NOUNS AND VERBS

Abstract nouns and verbs contribute to marshmallow sentences. Unnecessary abstractions dilute sentences and create unintelligible strings of
multisyllabic phrases. (The preceding sentence might simply have said,
"Stick to concrete nouns so that your sentences are clearer and contain
shorter words.") When writers use abstract rather than concrete words,
they may be responding to an innate need to dignify the subject—and
its author. Novice legal writers assume that important subjects need
serious-sounding vocabularies. That attitude leads a writer to say: "If
there is a continuation of this breach, my client will effect an immediate
termination of the mutually agreed-upon contract."

Legal prose that attempts to describe people acting, responding,
and asking is frequently inflated until no concrete action remains.
Nouns are shot with sugar, for example, inflating "car wreck" to "ve-
hicular collision." Action verbs disappear beneath a fog of "nominaliza-

tions." Writers twist verbs into important-sounding nouns so that "use" becomes "utilization," "add" becomes "the addition of," and "lack" becomes "deficiency." Somehow a four- or five-syllable fluff carries more weight than a tightly constructed noun and verb. Naturally those nominalizations create the need for even more words within the sentence to help them out. "You can improve your lack of punch" might end up in a court document as "One can ameliorate his or her deficiencies within the arena of 'punchivity.'"

Look for an abundance of multisyllabic words with the familiar endings listed below. The added syllable frequently hides an original action verb.

al	ion
ance	ity
ancy	ive
ant	ize
ence	tion

```
[Consternation] about low [attendance] has caused
[overreliance] on [publicity] by the officials.

Rewrite: Officials, concerned about few voters
attending the speeches, relied too heavily on
publicity rather than personal contact with the
voters.
```

PASSIVES

Legal writers hesitate to admit someone is doing something to someone else. The system preserves itself by masking the action taking place beneath the surface of its prose. "Plaintiff files this petition" becomes "This petition was filed by Plaintiff."

Endless paragraphs in memoranda begin "It was held that . . . ." *Who* held this soon-to-be-told exciting bit of news? Could it be that legal writers really do not know which court decided the issue? I doubt it. Perhaps the writer is saying that the particular court does not matter. More likely, the repetitive passives distinguish the legal landscape of documents because the writers are thinking their way into sentences, and then write them as the thought appears. Passive it came, and passive it shall be written.

Passive verbs take up extra room: "The form must be filled out by each defendant" takes nine words; "Each defendant must fill out the form" requires only seven. Plus the passive mutes the action; if the defendants need to fill something out, they need to act. The verb form should underscore that needed action, not dilute it.

Of course there are perfectly logical reasons for using an occasional passive verb, but those are deliberate choices; using the passive voice in legal writing probably results more from hurried and uninspired writing than from careful deliberation about verb forms.

Watch what happens when I switch from the passive into the active voice:

```
1. A copy of your letter of June 14 from John Smith
   to you has been received by this office. [We have
   received the copy of John Smith's June 14 letter
   to you.]
2. This proceeding was brought by Movant under 42
   U.S.C. [Movant brings (files? argues?) this pro-
   ceeding. 42 U.S.C.]
3. The highway flashers could be seen for a quarter
   of a mile. [A driver could see the highway signs a
   quarter of a mile away.]
```

■■■

Perhaps lawyers who produce marshmallow prose see themselves as philosophers; the issues are so grand, so sweeping, or so serious that only inflated abstractions can do them justice. Or perhaps marshmallow prose is the signature of lawyer-bureaucrats who believe no one will read the document anyway, so they might as well pump it up and puff it out.

Expert writers trim marshmallows and produce crisper, stronger prose.

The principle of law should receive the principal prose position. Why mute your point with a case name?

9
CASES AND CITATIONS WITHIN THE TEXT

Citations appear throughout legal instruments to document the authority behind an idea, a paraphrase, or a quotation. Even if attorneys conscientiously include only necessary citations, the placement of the case names and citations creates a major logistical problem for writers. Effective writers place necessary citations unobtrusively within the sentence structure.

Location of citations is a matter of politeness, actually. When you have worked on a legal problem, you can get so anxious to prove that you know your sources that you forget a reader must plow through the intrusion of the citation to find out what you are saying. Certainly, citations are a matter of convention, but a citation's greatest virtue is its documentation of the source of an idea that is clearly expressed in the sentence that readers are reading here and now.

Novice legal readers, initially faced with reams of archaic cases, train during the first weeks of law school to skim over both the names of the cases and the full citations that follow them to unravel the basic meaning of the sentence. Once they understand the prose message of the sentence, and perhaps the paragraph, students can reread the citation for its information, deciding whether the location of the court or type of court is significant. Accepting this reading style as merely another frustration of law school, students train their eyes to skim forward, double back, and skim forward again. Clients without legal backgrounds are constantly thwarted by references that overwhelm the message of the sentence. Occasionally, though, legal prose can be clear, understandable, perhaps even enjoyable—despite the documentation. It is written by masters of legal writing who have learned to evaluate citation-torn prose and who know the options around it.

PROBLEMS IN READABILITY

1. Using the case name as the *subject of the sentence* encourages readers to skip over both the case name and its citation. Thus, the reader ignores the subject of the sentence while hurrying on to find the verb. The writer expects the readers to hold the subject in abeyance while they read the rest of the sentence.

2. Attorneys who compose *several adjoining sentences* beginning with the case name and citation create a juggling act: the reader tries to keep several ideas in the air at the same time without focusing on any individual, concrete subject as the ideas go by. But the mental effort required to keep all those subjectless sentences afloat is too great, and readers must stop reading to mentally summarize several sentences. Thus, the readers are doing the work the writer has neglected. Although the readers have the option of reading each word and number in the case name and citation, most people cannot concentrate on both the legal concept and its authority at the same time:

> Burton v. National Bank of Commerce, 679 S.W.2d
> 115, 118 (Tex. App. 1984), held that a debtor must
> be notified at the time of a sale to remedy a de-
> fault. Tanenbaum v. Economics Laboratory, Inc.,
> 628 S.W.2d 769 (Tex. 1982), an earlier decision,
> discussed the options available to the creditor
> under Tex. Bus. Com. & Code Ann. §§9.504, .505
> (Tex. UCC) (Vernon Supp. 1985). Texas Business and
> Commercial Code governs the remedies of a secured
> party after default.

3. *Citations are not transitions*, so sentences beginning with case names necessarily are choppy and detached sentences. Lacking transitions, the stacked sentences force readers to guess at the connections between sentences. Hearing this complaint about case names, one attorney argued, "But they're the *point* of the paragraph!" But isn't it the principle of law, and not the citation, that is usually the essence of the sentence? Perhaps if an attorney wants the court to be overwhelmed by 152 previous courts that have agreed with the interpretation, then

paragraphs of prominent case names are indeed "the point." Occasionally, a partner will ask an associate or clerk for a quick list of all applicable cases on a legal point without asking the writer to tie the cases together or come to a conclusion. Other than those exceptions, however, the principle of law should be given prominence within the sentence structure; case names and citations can be relegated to supplementary positions.

4. If writers use a case name as the subject of the sentence and follow it with its full citation, the *subject is unnecessarily separated from its verb*.

> The same considerations dictate a contrary rule
> for those who voluntarily place themselves in the
> role of a "professional rescuer." Firemen (both
> professional and voluntary), <u>Buchanan v. Prickett
> & Sons</u>, 203 Neb. 684, 689, 279 N.W.2d 855 (1979),
> policemen, <u>Mounsey v. Ellard</u>, 363 Mass. 693, 297
> N.E.2d 43 (1973), security guards, <u>Krueger v. City
> of Anaheim</u>, 130 Cal. App. 3d 166, 181 Cal. Rptr.
> 631 (Cal. 1982), and even doctors, <u>Carter v. Tay-
> lor Diving & Salvage Co.</u>, 341 F. Supp. 628, 631
> (E.D. La. 1972), <u>aff'd</u>, 470 F.2d 995 (5th Cir.
> 1973), have all been held subject to the singular
> exception to the "Rescue Doctrine."

An alternative to the tortured structure above might be a generalized introduction that allows the subject and verb proximity: "Courts have held a variety of professionals subject to the singular exception to the 'Rescue Doctrine': . . . [the citations could be listed here with each profession following the respective case name and citation, in parentheses]."

Although the commas before and after the citation usually help experienced readers understand where to pick up the sentence again, repetition of the subject-citation sentence pattern can create leap-frog reading, in which the eye is forced to skip constantly over numbers and abbreviations. If you will reexamine the examples above, you will see that long, or numerous, citations are not easily skipped.

5. If writers place the citation for one sentence at the *end* of that sentence and *begin* the next sentence with another case name and citation, a reader's eyes will frequently skip from the end of the first sentence and land, unexpectedly, somewhere in the middle of the second

sentence. The puzzled reader must begin with the first sentence again, wasting time searching for the one period, of the many used within citations, that signals the end of the first idea:

> The court's goal in deciding to exercise or de-
> cline jurisdiction is to render a forum where the
> trial will best serve the convenience of the par-
> ties and the ends of justice, Koster v. (American)
> Lumbermans Mut. Casualty Co., 330 U.S. 518, 527
> (1947). Gulf Oil Corp. v. Gilbert, 330 U.S. 501
> (1947), established a two-step procedure for de-
> ciding whether to dismiss a case on forum non con-
> veniens grounds.

ALTERNATIVES

Once sensitized to readability problems created by case names and citations, legal writers can train themselves to deemphasize them. In most sentences the alternative is a simple shift of emphasis within the sentence that allows readers to follow the discussion more easily. If the citations are not "the point," then writers can incorporate the name of the court into their text and leave the full citation for the end of the sentence:

> The United States Supreme Court, again that year,
> established a two-step procedure for deciding
> whether to dismiss a case on forum non conveniens
> grounds. Gulf Oil v. Gilbert, 330 U.S. 501 (1947).

This solution also avoids suggesting that a case, rather than a court, decides an issue:

> Misleading: Piper Aircraft Co. v. Reyno, 454 U.S.
> 235 (1981), held that a judge could claim a for-
> eign forum to be adequate only if the entire case
> and all the parties come within the jurisdiction
> of that forum.

> Correction: The United States Supreme Court held
> that a judge could claim a foreign forum to be ad-
> equate only if the entire case and all the parties
> come within the jurisdiction of that forum. Piper
> Aircraft Co. v. Reyno, 454 U.S. 235 (1981).

However, if those "dangling citations" at the end of sentences threaten to create additional confusion, writers may have to tuck the citation within a prepositional phrase, separated from the rest of the sentence by appropriate commas:

> The United States Supreme Court established a two-step procedure, in <u>Gulf Oil Corp. v. Gilbert</u>, 330 U.S. 501 (1947), for deciding whether to dismiss a case on forum non conveniens grounds.

A reasonable argument against the court name used both in the text and within the following citation is that the court name becomes redundant. However, readers skimming legal arguments generally skip over the citation until they find it necessary to return and concentrate on it.

An additional problem with tucking citations into prepositional phrases is their length. Citations within prepositional phrases are unobtrusive only if they contain short citations and do not create too much distance between the subject and verb.

Finally, you can vary sentence structure so that not all sentences begin with case names, unless the name of the case is the most important information in the sentence. Case names and citations cause less trouble when they are used to support a fully developed sentence. The specialized sentence structure created by case names is particularly distracting at the beginning of paragraphs, where readers expect a succinct introduction into the concept of the new paragraph, rather than a recitation of names and numbers. A quick editing of the topic sentences before you submit a document will help the reader follow your discussion, undeterred by the documentation.

■■■

Note: An El Paso attorney sent me a page from a recent opinion and asked if I could "make heads or tails" of it. Interestingly, only three sentences on the entire page began with a subject other than a case name. It might prove a useful exercise for you to return to a piece of your own prose and edit it by relocating case names. You may discover that you have neglected to articulate the basic concepts underlying your citation of cases.

Expert writers experiment with their sentences, moving coordinate ideas to subordinate positions and back again, until the hierarchy of the sentence emphasizes its meaning.

10
COORDINATION AND SUBORDINATION
Defining Relationships

A corollary to the traditional idea that "writing reveals thinking" is that "muddled thinking produces muddled writing." According to this axiom, if writers have a clear grasp of their information, their writing will also be clear. I've always wondered if proponents of such thoughts believe draft sentences, rather than revised sentences, reflect that clarity.

Only as we tumble our words onto the page or into a dictating machine do we begin to see our story, our argument, take shape. The time to focus on the relationships between the disparate parts of our document is during the reading of a first draft. Only then can we see that point one is independent of point two, but that points three and four are inexorably tied to the outcome of point two and thus dependent.

Some sentences create confusion when their elements are not organized into coordinate and subordinate structures that parallel the substantive relationships. Each of the sentences in the examples reveals this confusion between coordination and subordination on the sentence level, a confusion that readers can also apply to the larger segments of their documents, for instance, major headings and subheadings, topic sentences of paragraphs, and divisions within an argument.

To *coordinate* means to make "of equal rank or importance." A writer can coordinate full sentences and create compound sentences that reflect balance or contrast:

```
The bankruptcy court can offer debtors a "fresh
start," but the freshness is nevertheless burdened
by remaining tax debts.
```

Writers also coordinate parts of sentences: adjective to adjective, verb to verb, clause to clause, or sentence to sentence:

```
Federal, state, and even employment taxes, as well
as student loans, follow a bankrupt, reminding the
debtor that not all creditors disappear and en-
couraging the debtor to become responsible for
both a slice of the past as well as the present
and future.
```

In the sentence above, the writer has created a series of coordinates:

```
1.  • federal taxes,
    • state taxes, and
    • employment taxes, as well as
    • student loans
2.  (they) follow • reminding the debtor and
                  • encouraging the debtor
3.  responsible for both • a slice of the past as
                           well as
                         • the present and future
```

Not all ideas are equal; not all sentence elements are either. Thus, *subordination* means "the act of placing in a lower class or rank." To employ subordination, writers traditionally choose the idea and word(s) of primary importance; afterward, they relegate the other words and clauses to lesser relationships with the main idea. Subordination helps specify logical relationships between words and clauses: time, place, manner, condition, cause, concession, parts of the whole. Without subordination, all sentences would end up in the sing-song balance of preschoolers: "Jimmy loves Mary . . . Mary loves Tommy . . . We hate school." Using subordination, writers can improve the ease with which readers can mentally organize a series of ideas by providing a hierarchy of importance to the elements.

```
Although many critics argue that bankruptcy is a
haven for irresponsible debtors who file repeated
```

```
bankruptcies, cold statistics reveal that fewer
than 5 percent of the petitioners have been in
bankruptcy court before. More important, many
of those 5 percent are refiling their original
pleadings.
```

In this example, the important news is the statistics, although the writer introduces the news with the old theory. The first clause is dependent, introduced by the adverb "although," which relegates it to the subordinate. The second sentence is equally important to the writer and is placed as a coordinate, complete sentence. To make the statistics less important, the writer need only reverse the subordinate clauses:

```
Contrary to the statistics that suggest only
5 percent of the petitioners in bankruptcy are
repeaters, critics continue to argue that peti-
tioners use bankruptcy as a haven for irresponsi-
ble debtors. These critics, who find it difficult
to understand how petitioners are not counted as
refilers when they are usually converting one
chapter into another, remain convinced that the
system is protecting deadbeats.
```

In this rewrite, the emphasis turns on the critics and their opinions rather than on the statistics. The intent of the writer would determine which material belongs in independent positions and which is relegated to dependent, subordinate positions.

Let us take a look at five sentences that suffer from a confusion between coordination and subordination. This first example exemplifies the problem:

```
Each issue in the proceeding was covered, treated
as affirmed, reversed, or modified, and when there
was a modification, the modification was stated.
```

As written, the subject of the first independent clause ("issue") is followed by four parallel and equal verbs, four coordinate verbs:

```
each issue • was covered
              • treated as affirmed
              • reversed or
              • modified
```

The sense of the sentence, however, follows not a straight coordinate path but a coordinate-subordinate one. "Each issue" was *covered* and *treated*—two main, coordinate verbs. How the issue was treated is detailed by three subordinate verbs:

```
each issue • was covered
           • was treated as • affirmed
                            • reversed or
                            • modified
```

One way to help the sentence structure follow the writer's intention would be to include a coordinating conjunction ("and") after the first verb. The two main verbs are thus conjoined and equal; the reader has no trouble following the relationship despite the following subordination because an "as" introduces the substructure:

```
Each issue was covered and treated as affirmed,
reversed, or modified.
```

To reduce the added confusion that the second full clause creates, the writer could separate it into a second sentence:

```
Each issue was covered and treated as affirmed,
reversed, or modified. If there was a modifica-
tion, the modification was stated.
```

Let us look at a second example of coordinate-subordinate confusion:

```
We suggest you monitor the account, reestablish
the credit line, check a little further on his
commercial credit line, and ride herd on the
customer.
```

According to the grammar and punctuation of this sentence, the writer is asking the reader to go to work in four ways:

```
We suggest you • monitor
               • reestablish
               • check
               • ride herd
```

But what does "monitor" mean if not reestablishing, checking, and riding herd? Again, these verbs are subordinate to the main verb; it comprises them:

```
We suggest you monitor (by) • establishing
                               • checking
                               • riding herd
```

Changing the last three verbs from verbs that *parallel* (coordinate) the main verb into gerunds (*ing* verbs that function as nouns) that *follow* the preposition ("by") establishes the desired relationship. Another option to retain the subordinate nature of the three verbs would be to split the main verb from its smaller units with a colon:

```
We suggest you monitor the account: reestablish
the credit line, check a little further on his
commercial credit, and ride herd on the customer.
```

The colon warns the reader that a list, an illustration, or a summation is to follow.

The next two sentences also fail coordinate-subordinate scrutiny:

```
In this case, problems in all three areas of con-
cern, absenteeism, disregard for company policy,
and, primarily, inadequate ability to perform the
job, have arisen.
```

```
We selected three states, Texas, Illinois, and
Pennsylvania, because they vary in interest-
ing ways that we believe might be important to
bankruptcy.
```

Here are writers who know what they mean to say but haven't *seen* what they were saying. Comma strings need to follow accepted usage (signal interruption, divide lists, divide independent clauses with conjunctions, introduce and close conjunctive adverbs that interrupt a sentence).

In the first example, problems in "three areas" have arisen. The detailed areas are a part of the larger entity, "three areas of concern." As originally written, "three areas" is grammatically parallel to its smaller units, the detailed breakdown. The following rewrite distinguishes between the whole and its parts:

> In this case, problems have arisen in all three
> areas of concern: absenteeism; disregard for com-
> pany policy; and, primarily, inadequate ability to
> perform the job.

Moving the verb closer to its subject exposes the internal inconsistency. The addition of a colon anticipates the list. Semicolons are necessary because one element of the list itself contains commas; the semicolons function therefore as large commas, separating equal items that contain their own punctuation.

The second example about the states is slightly more problematic but contains the same error. The names of the specific states are subordinate to the comprising phrase, "three states." As written, the list is equal to, coordinates with, its larger unit, "three states," creating a logical fallacy. A whole is not equal to each one of its parts. Unlike the first example, the writer does not want to move the detailed list to another location within the sentence, because the list needs to follow the wider generalization "states." Perhaps a shifting of the adverbial clause highlights the writer's intention:

> Because they vary in interesting ways that we be-
> lieve might be important to a generalized theory,
> we selected three states: Texas, California, and
> New York.

Here again the generalization, the larger entity, is followed by a colon and list of subordinate elements. These subordinate elements are in themselves coordinate (three equal states) and thus connected by commas. If writers consider the colons too stark or intrusive, they can place the state names within a prepositional phrase, a position that also signals subordination:

> Because they vary in interesting ways that we be-
> lieve might be important to a generalized theory,
> we selected the three states of Texas, California,
> and New York.

Parallelism is created by both the punctuation and the grammar of the sentence. This next sentence is an example of nonparallel grammar that muddles the distinction between coordinate elements:

> For example, if the issue is whether the employee
> voluntarily left the school, the memorandum should

```
contain a statement of facts that the employee
left (and was not discharged), concerning the
circumstances (to see whether the employee left
voluntarily or involuntarily), and as to the rea-
son(s) for leaving (to determine the question of
good cause).
```

If readers attempt to list the details the memorandum should contain, the result looks like this:

```
memorandum should contain • findings
                          • concerning the circum-
                            stances
                          • as to the reasons for
                            leaving
```

Maybe you could follow that directive, but most readers would still be puzzling about what the writer wanted because the details are not grammatically parallel. For instance, if writers want noun forms after the verb "should contain," they would change the list:

```
memo should contain • findings
                    • a description of circum-
                      stances and
                    • reasons for leaving
```

The list does not have to contain noun forms, but if one element in it is a noun, they should all be nouns.

Keeping sentence elements parallel—as coordinates or subordinates—will highlight the relationships within your argument.

We all know someone we respect as a great writer. That writer can teach us, if we'll analyze how the writing is great.

11
EXAMINING OTHER PROFESSIONAL PROSE

Good writers read other good writers to help them analyze effective prose and then experiment with the rhetorical devices they discover.

Toward that end, I offer two recent examples of successful legal writing: the first is a section of a brief, and the second is an opinion letter to the administrative law judge at the Public Utility Commission. Both were written to persuade their audiences, and I believe both were successful for similar reasons.

APPRECIATING A MAESTRO'S TOUCH

C. Defendants Fail to Justify New Mexico's Discrimination Against Interstate Commerce

In their Brief on Remand, Defendants attempt to justify or explain away New Mexico's discrimination against interstate commerce in water. Their efforts fail.

To begin with, Defendants suggest that the Supreme Court in *Sporhase* approved equally substantial discrimination by Nebraska. Defendants' Brief on Remand at pp. 12–13, 15–16. This suggestion is erroneous. The Court found that Nebraska's export laws "may well be no more strict" than its in-state regulations. 459 U.S. at 926. Nebraska's in-state regulations are "severe"; Nebraska requires flow meters on every well, specifies the amounts of water per acre that can be used, and prohibits intrastate transfers except between lands controlled by the same user. *Id.* at 955–956. New Mexico, in contrast, does not require meters, does not limit per acre water use, and does not severely limit intrastate transfers of existing rights. In fact, protection of prior rights is the only limit that New Mexico places on in-state transfers of existing rights, and New Mexico counts on the marketplace in those rights to transfer water from irrigation to urban uses. See generally Defendants' Exhibit F, pp. 200–208; R. Supp. 138; Reynolds' Statement, pp. 21–23.[1]

In this example, Professor Pieter Schenkkan uses three stylistic techniques worth investigating: first, his effective *transitions* pull readers through the argument; second, he twice breaks his paragraphs with unusually *short sentences* that deliver an undercut punch; and third, he makes optimum use of *parallel sentence structure.*

Transitions

Schenkkan uses two transitional devices: traditional word transitions and repetition. His word transitions signal location in the material (*"To begin"*), signal contrast (*"New Mexico, in contrast"*), and signal a shift from general to specific (*"In fact"*). Each of these overt transitions works directly; each presents an explicit road sign signaling where the reader stands in relationship to the rest of the text.

Repetition

Effective writers can repeat important words throughout a document to provide additional transitions and create emphasis. Schenkkan uses a more subtle form of repetition—he repeats important syllables; that is, he repeats a piece of a word containing a major concept from one sentence to the next sentence. This repetition functions as a sophisticated transition, connecting sentences with word sounds rather than words. He changes a strong verb (*"Defendants suggest"*) into a noun (*"This suggestion"*). He repeats a verb from the heading (*"Fail to Justify"*) in the text and even adds a synonym to it, doubling its effectiveness (*"attempt to justify or explain away"*). If readers had not already focused on the message the first time, they are subliminally bombarded with it the

---

[1] Plaintiffs' Reply on Mootness and Facial Unconstitutionality, City of El Paso v. Reynolds, No. 80-730HB (D.N.M. filed Mar. 19, 1984).

second time. The repeated syllables create a subtext that persuades through sophisticated repetition that is not really perceptible unless readers study the paragraph for rhetorical devices; the subtext, however, adds a parallel layer of reinforcement for the main text, emphasizing the primary points.

Parallel structure

The most memorable English prose develops through parallelism, the repeated use of any piece of sentence structure from prepositional phrases to entire independent clauses. This repetition of form is used more frequently than repetition of words to establish a cadence, which makes it a perfect form for speeches (and introductions to important arguments):

> And so, my fellow Americans, ask not what your country can do for you; ask what you can do for your country.[2]

> We shall not flag or fail. We shall go on to the end. We shall fight in France, we shall fight on the seas and oceans, we shall fight with growing confidence and growing strength in the air, we shall defend our island, whatever the cost may be, we shall fight on the beaches, we shall fight on the landing grounds, we shall fight in the fields and in the streets, we shall fight in the hills; we shall never surrender.[3]

The cadence catches the attention of the listener, and the reader, through a strict adherence to pattern. Whether writers use parallel nouns or verbs or phrases, the form must remain consistent for it to work. But done correctly, it does work and is worth the effort.

In his paragraph, Schenkkan parallels the verbs and objects after the nouns/subjects—not just in the first list for Nebraska, but again in the second list for New Mexico. Indeed, he not only creates the initial parallel (*"requires flow meters, specifies amounts of water, prohibits transfers"*) but repeats that parallel in the second series: parallel of a parallel.

The power of this paragraph might have been achieved in other ways—writers could approach the original case summaries and facts and notes about this issue and develop different points or see the

---

[2] President John F. Kennedy, Inaugural Address (Jan. 20, 1961).
[3] Winston S. Churchill, Speech on Dunkirk at the House of Commons (June 4, 1940).

argument in a different slant of light. Any writer could have changed the sequence, the blatant transitions, and certainly the rhythm of the prose. There are endless varieties of approaches to the same paragraph, and probably the result could be equally as good, as long as the writers consciously applied themselves to the task of producing effective prose.

Short sentences

Another prose technique is to vary sentence length. Schenkkan places two wham-bang punches into sentences of only three and five words:

```
Their efforts fail.
This suggestion is erroneous.
```

These short sentences, which contain his major arguments, call attention to themselves by their brevity. *"Their efforts fail"* follows a twenty-word introductory sentence. Similarly, *"This suggestion is erroneous"* presents a striking contrast to the two long sentences on either side of it. Schenkkan has resisted the temptation, to which most of us give in so easily, to elaborate the major point with qualifications, discussions, and definitions. When I examine my own paragraphs for the major ideas, I usually find them linked, like railroad cars, with all the detail I thought so important to the idea that I did not want it separated from the kernel, the train's engine. I thus unwittingly defeat my purpose.

No one, however, suggests that all sentences in legal writing should *always* contain only five words; choppy, jolty prose may work for *USA Today*, but it is not appropriate for legal writing. The lesson is that an occasional short sentence is not only appropriate but also dynamite when it is crafted carefully.

FINDING TIME TO "FIDDLE"

No one is so naive as to believe Schenkkan produced this paragraph in his first draft. He worked on the material after he developed the legal concepts, after the first draft, and maybe even after the tenth draft. This argument was apparently important enough that he felt justified taking the time to massage his word choice and sentence structure so that it would carry as much power as the law that his sentence is describing.

In a second example of good writing, Gus Ankum, an analyst at the Public Utility Commission of Texas (PUC), produced this response to AT&T's argument before the PUC:

AT&T does not, in a systematic way, address any of the factors traditionally used in economic analysis (see above). Nowhere does AT&T discuss what their unit cost is versus that of smaller carriers. Nowhere does AT&T expound on the benefits from scale economies in production, distribution, capital raising, or promotion. Yet, it is exactly these topics that fill the larger part of any textbook on industrial organization and that in the minds of their authors are instrumental in explaining industry structure and performance—the expressed purpose of this proceeding. The omission is conspicuous.

As you can tell, this paragraph uses many of the same rhetorical techniques as the first example.

Transitions

The one explicit transition in this paragraph is startling. "*Yet*" creates an interesting break in the prose rhythm. Within the structure of the paragraph, it operates as a fulcrum: the first three sentences list what AT&T is not doing; the "*Yet*" breaks the paragraph and its contents in two, both signaling the contrast and introducing two sentences that explain what AT&T should have done.

Repetition

The paragraph achieves its force through the use of negatives, beginning with "*AT&T does not.*" Then Ankum manipulates the specific negative "*does not*" into the global "*nowhere*," places it at the beginning of the second sentence, and thus emphasizes the negative. He repeats "*nowhere*" as an eye-catching beginning to the third sentence, creating a predictable rhythm that builds momentum into the contrasting sentences that follow "*Yet.*"

Short sentences

No one could fault Ankum for too many short sentences; indeed, the fourth sentence is unusually long. But the concluding sentence, which follows the long, explanatory fourth sentence, carries a TKO punch. It contains only four deadly words ("*The omission is conspicuous*"). The variety of sentence lengths, like Schenkkan's above, adds additional power to the paragraph.

12
EMULATING THE PRO'S PROSE
Stylistic Consciousness

Attorneys who spend their days and nights reading legal documents may assume without realizing it that legal arguments and fact statements are somehow divorced from the rest of the world and its vocabulary, that they cannot waste time reading outside the law. But this premise is flawed: legal issues revolve around real people and their questions, problems, and solutions. To write about them, effective legal writers must depend on a language and sentence structure whose essence derives from that larger world. Legal language is only another layer of the rich language and intricate structure that nonlegal readers can have reinforced every time they read. Legal writers need to read about history, journalism, the classics, science, even economics, so that they can come in touch with the larger world again.

There is an old joke about a golfer who has a pronounced hook to his swing. He first considers taking lessons but decides instead to concentrate on his problem and practice frequently. He practices, all right, and develops such an unshakable hook that even his putts roll to the left. The point, obviously, is that practice without instruction does not enhance art; it merely solidifies initial problems. Legal writers who read only legal materials reinforce a dense and daunting style repeated by other legal writers who believe "that's the way it's always been."

Theorists still argue whether writers learn by reading, by imitating others, or by trial and error. Learning may finally be the result of all these techniques. What I am suggesting is that legal writers take a conscious look at the writers they judge as good and try to apply these successful stylistic techniques to legal writing. They might discover a fresh perspective, a technique that allows them to break traditional formulas of idiosyncratic legal analysis.

BULKY QUOTATIONS

One continuing problem in legal writing, for instance, is the bulky quotations that create major hurdles to reading. Although legal argument depends on authority, that necessity should not become an excuse to drop quotations into a text with no introduction or concluding discussion. If that is a problem in your writing, you can look, for instance, to Annie Dillard, naturalist-theologian-poet, to examine how she skillfully incorporates secondary material into a text that is finally her own, making frequent references to outside authority as the underpinning for her discussions. *Pilgrim at Tinker Creek* is a contemporary glimpse into nature, similar to Thoreau's *Walden*. If you get a chance to read Dillard's book, you will discover after only a chapter or two that you've been casually introduced to dozens of scientists, naturalists, philosophers, theologians, optometrists, etc. Look at two paragraphs from *Pilgrim at Tinker Creek*:

> I open my eyes and I see dark, muscled forms curl out of water, with flapping gills and flattened eyes. I close my eyes and I see stars, deep stars giving way to deeper stars, deeper stars bowing to deepest stars at the crown of an infinite cone.
>
> "Still," writes Van Gogh in a letter, "a great deal of light falls on everything." If we are to be blinded by darkness, we are also blinded by light. When too much light falls on everything, a special terror results. Peter Freuchen describes the notorious kayak sickness to which Greenland Eskimos are prone. "The Greenland fjords are peculiar for the spells of completely quiet weather. . . . The kayak hunter must sit in his boat without stirring a finger so as not to scare the shy seals away. . . . The reflex [of the sun] from the mirror-like water hypnotizes him . . . and all of a sudden it is as if he were floating in a bottomless void, sinking, sinking, sinking . . . ." Some hunters are especially

cursed with this panic, and bring ruin and sometimes starvation to their families.[1]

Dillard has used both van Gogh and Freuchen to develop her earlier point about darkness and light in such a way that the two direct quotations become a part of her text, an integral thread in her own fabric of expression. The quotations do not stand alone as mere book and letter summaries, as is frequently the case in legal writing; readers have no trouble moving from her textual observations to the explanatory quotations, because the quotations add to what she has already said and anticipated.

Memorandum and brief writers can take a lesson here and compare their own abilities to incorporate secondary source material. They will not get that contrast if they compare their use of quotations to that of most other legal writers.

KEEPING TRACK OF GREAT PROSE

In the eighteenth and nineteenth centuries, people frequently carried pocket notebooks into which they wrote observations, recorded conversations, and copied interesting descriptions they picked up through reading. Later they used these notes as the basis for their own writing. Nathaniel Hawthorne is an obvious example, with a notebook entry that describes his daughter at play in the woods; the scene appears almost verbatim in his description of impish Pearl in *The Scarlet Letter*. Perhaps it would not be a bad idea to borrow that habit—a thin spiral notebook fits easily into a jacket pocket or pocketbook. You could copy sentences from *The New Yorker* or novels, jot down conversations, and even have a place to keep those stray thoughts that strike you as genius but frequently fade before you can do anything with them. It is a variation on highlighting newspaper articles and books, a practice that may actually work for the well-organized writer. Unfortunately, most of us pile those original articles into stacks and maybe get around to hiding them even deeper inside a file cabinet. There, they remain out of sight and are too much trouble to retrieve. The notebook, on the other hand, keeps these jewels together and available for quick retrieval when writers need them.

---

[1] ANNIE DILLARD, PILGRIM AT TINKER CREEK 22 (Bantam Books 1975).

Today's technology allows us to open a file on the computer and type in interesting examples of paragraphs and bits of sentences. My "Samples" file is a mishmash of thoughts on a variety of topics—but each sentence is crafted so that I can emulate the structure to present my own ideas.

LEGAL EXAMPLES USING NONLEGAL PATTERNS

In the paragraphs below, two legal writers have experimented with the style of authors beyond the world of law: they have taken a paragraph or sentence and rewritten it, retaining the word order and rhythm but replacing the history or science content with legal issues. The idea in the two experiments is to pattern a legal issue on some example of outstanding writing; I chose the outside references, and the two attorneys molded their ideas into the sentence pattern of the originals. The paragraph below is from Patricia Nelson Limerick's outstanding book that details the human story of the expansion of the American West, *The Legacy of Conquest*:

> Western history is a story structured by the drawing of lines and the marking of borders. From macrocosm to microcosm, from imperial struggles for territory to the parceling out of townsite claims, Western American history was an effort first to draw lines dividing the West into manageable units of property and then to persuade people to treat those lines with respect.[2]

You'll notice that the first sentence uses gerunds after the preposition, creating a rhythmic parallel ("the *drawing*," "the *marking*"). The second sentence's structure develops with a string of introductory, parallel prepositional phrases: from (large) to (small), from (large) to (small). The main clause develops through a second parallel: "first to draw lines . . . and then to persuade . . . ." These lively coordinates establish a rhythm that marches the reader through the metaphor/reality she is defining.

Scot Powe, author of the multi-award-winning *American Broadcasting and the First Amendment* (1987), experimented with the

---

[2] Patricia N. Limerick, The Legacy of Conquest 55 (1987).

same sentence structure applied to his topic of broadcast regulation, added a conclusion, and produced this model of legal writing for this publication:

> Broadcast regulation is a matrix of public service and localism. From the Fairness Doctrine to the allocation of television licenses, from Herbert Hoover to Jimmy Carter, broadcast regulation was a conscious policy first to maximize the public welfare by providing essential information and second to encourage national diversity through the celebration of local uniqueness. The matrix, however, is built on theoretical foundations that weaken significantly when they confront the laws of economics.

In this example, Powe maintains both the cadence and the coordination of Limerick's original two sentences. Look at the elements of the sentence: Powe's vocabulary retains Limerick's sophistication—but no one would complain about legal jargon or archaic language, because, although sophisticated, the words are grouped into easily understood units and thus convey readily available meaning. It is nonsense, then, to generalize that good legal writing uses simple words—attorneys have a wide vocabulary and need only use it appropriately. The power and richness of the English language work together with the legal concept to produce memorable writing.

Powe's sentences, like Limerick's, are long—especially the second one—and complex. Here good legal writing does not depend on short and choppy sentences for clarity but rather depends on frequent closure and visual cues to internal coherence. It is not, then, that legal writing has to slip to the lowest common denominator to be clear. Rather, sentences can contain sophisticated language and complex structure—if they are not replete with embedded, run-on clauses or archaic redundancies. This example is proof that legal writers, striving for clarity or precision, need not limit themselves to a restricted number of sentence structures; nor should they ignore their writing problems altogether under the excuse that changing their style would make their writing less succinct or precise.

A second example of writing that legal writers might benefit by reading is *The Lives of a Cell.* In this book a scientist, Lewis Thomas, has addressed a complicated topic, one full of abstractions and theory and minute detail; he has nevertheless created a book so informative that college students are asked to read it in both writing and biology classes:

> [S]urely this is the toughest membrane imaginable in the universe, opaque to probability, impermeable to death. We are the delicate part, transient and vulnerable as cilia.[3]

Thomas creates these memorable sentences through the use of short descriptive clauses tacked to the end of the sentences after the nouns they modify and expand. The tough membrane is described at the sentence's conclusion, almost as a toss-in phrase, as "*opaque to probability.*" Then again, rather than the traditional conjunctive *and* to separate two adjectival descriptions, Thomas uses only the comma. That leaves the phrase "*impermeable to death*" out there all by itself. It is the lack of conjunction and the placement of the descriptions that are eye-catching; the recognition that membranes would not allow even death becomes all the more startling because the sentence in which Thomas explains it is also startling. The second sentence also catches us unaware: comparing humans to the hairs of the membrane, Thomas uses a traditional ellipsis to introduce the understood juxtaposition of the delicate cilia to us ("*We are the delicate part; [we are as] transient and vulnerable as cilia*"). The challenge to legal writers to create explanatory, vivid metaphors is no more overwhelming than it is to scientists.

Sanford Levinson, author of the thought-provoking *Constitutional Faith* (1988), used Thomas' passage as a pattern to develop his own two sentences concerning individual rights and contributed the following example for this publication:

> Surely the dominating impulse of the state is often to maintain its "security," an impulse at once impermeable to evidence that it is not threatened and exaggerating the probability of attack. Individual rights and ordinary human liberties are often too fragile to survive, as transient and vulnerable as delicate limestone that is worn away by the relentless pounding of mighty rivers.

---

[3] LEWIS THOMAS, THE LIVES OF A CELL 8 (1974).

Levinson maintains the double modifiers after "impulse" but separates them with the traditional conjunction and then reinstates the omitted "as" in the second sentence to define the rights and liberties "*as* transient and vulnerable *as* delicate limestone." Levinson transforms Thomas' original into an expanded literary metaphor. Legal questions involve the mighty, the powerful, the threatened, the angry, and the needed. Should not legal language echo that vitality? Levinson's flourish may not be appropriate in a motion for summary judgment, but surely in the routine papers that flow in and out of law offices there is the *possibility* of lively prose.

■■■

Using others' sentence structures, language—and even ideas— is not foreign to the world of the law. A conscious attempt to integrate outside sources into legal writing may be a foreign exercise, however. These conscious adaptations become more than an exercise if they lay the foundation for a developing style.

13

DELIBERATE SENTENCE STRUCTURE

Most writers create sentences while they are thinking about the content; sentence structure itself is thus incidental and frequently repetitive. But it does not have to be that way. If legal writers can identify one sympathetic fact, one on-point holding, one persuasive concept in their memorandum or brief that contains the essence of their discussion or argument, those deliberate writers can massage that element until it states, concisely and memorably, just what readers will remember after they walk away from the document. Maybe the remaining sentences have to be tossed onto the page in a rush to the courthouse, but the main concept needs to be pampered, babied, and cajoled until it speaks not only to the logical mind but subliminally to the unconscious through elegance, simplicity, and the surprising rhythm of the language.

Traditional English sentence structure begins with a noun that is followed by the verb that can be completed with an object. Traditional *legal* writing, in contrast, begins with an adverbial clause that qualifies, quantifies, denies, introduces, or limits, and then finally concedes a main noun-verb-object. If you were to examine your last document, you might discover that you leaned exclusively on these introductory adverbial clauses:

```
When the defendant asked for extra time and
pointed to his attempts to contact all the parties
without success, this court refused to consider
the extension.
```

Or you might discover that you used only two sentence patterns throughout. Another typical discovery is thirty sentences beginning, "The court held that . . . ." As depressing as these discoveries may be, you probably will not want to rework your sentences just to create variety, unless a review of your sentence structures puts even you to sleep. Nevertheless, recognizing and acknowledging your habits of sentence structure can help when you discover a pressing need for memorable prose; you will become aware of your typical structure. Then you can apply one of the options for sentence structure.

Investigating the options for sentence structure is more than an academic exercise; word order in sentences creates emphasis, heralding the hierarchy that helps readers understand the sentence parts' relative importance. Watch what happens when I switch the structure of two sentences:

> ```
> In Frazier, the most recent Third Circuit case to
> discuss this standard, the court relied on Rotolo
> and Hall to hold that some of the claims before
> the court were sufficiently specific, while others
> were not.
> ```

The organization of these sentences sends a signal that *Frazier*'s reliance on *Rotolo* and *Hall* is the major point because the subject, verb, and object are "court," "relied on," and "*Rotolo* and *Hall*." It could be that reliance on other holdings *was* the important issue. But what if the point of these two sentences were that the Third Circuit had applied the standard and that this application had been recent? Then the writer would need to shift the sentences a bit:

> ```
> The most recent Third Circuit case to discuss this
> standard decided it is possible for the court to
> rule that some of the claims are sufficiently
> specific while others are not. Frazier, [full ci-
> tation] (relying on Rotolo and Hall).
> ```

The move of "recent Third Circuit" to the front of the sentences emphasizes the court; shifting the secondary sources into an abbreviated citation moves them from major textual consideration into lesser documentation.

Another possibility for these sentences is to reorder them to emphasize the holding of the case:

```
The court can rule that some of the claims are
sufficiently specific while others are not.
Frazier, [citation].
```

Each rewrite shifts the emphasis of the sentence from the underlying policy cases to the holding or the court; in these original sentences, the holding was supposed to be the essence the writer wanted readers to understand and remember, but the sentence structure defeated the sentence's purpose.

No one system of arrangement can work for all sentences, but the first and last words of sentences are the most effective. Writers who have pinpointed important information and arguments might try this technique: articulate, aloud, what their readers need to remember after reading the whole document; after hearing themselves actually *say* the important sentence, good writers strategically move that information into positions that emphasize it.

Let's take a list of facts from the notes of a client interview in which two brothers are arguing the question of tenancy in common.

```
• Melvin and Otis are brothers, inherited land to
  share from Uncle Otto
• Melvin moved onto Mount Olympus property and con-
  verted family residence into ski resort
• Melvin spent $2.7 million on hillside slopes,
  $40,000 on necessary roof repairs; Otis visited,
  saw project progress
• Melvin paid mortgage payments and half of the
  taxes but did not pay Otis rent
• Otis paid the other half of the property taxes
• Otis has decided to develop property into fishing
  resort
```

The writer preparing a statement of facts could anticipate any number of legal arguments: consent and implied consent, necessary maintenance versus expansion spending, the doctrine of waste and ameliorated waste, and the issue of control between non-active and active co-owners in the rights of improved property.

First suppose that brother Otis has hired you to get Melvin and his resort off the mutually owned land. After you have organized your legal arguments, you realize that this introductory paragraph in the statement of facts is pivotal. Hurriedly, however, you draft a paragraph that follows your notes from the initial interview:

```
Uncle Otto died, leaving brothers Otis and Melvin
as heirs to his property. Melvin moved into the
old family lodge and turned it into a ski resort.
He did not pay Otis rent for his share of the
property but paid the mortgage and half of the
property taxes. He spent almost $2 million on re-
pairs and improvements, but Otis did not formally
approve these improvements. Otis maintained an ac-
tive interest in the property, visiting it often
and paying his half of the property taxes.
```

Unfortunately, that draft paragraph does not reveal any tension or anticipate any of the legal arguments that will develop from these facts.

Why not rewrite the first sentences to emphasize Otis' right to share in the land and decisions about it? A *relative clause (which, who, that, whose* followed by a verbal) can combine two ideas, emphasizing the first:

```
Otis and Melvin, who inherited the land after
Uncle Otto died, own the property on Mount Olympus
and are tenants in common. Otis allowed Melvin to
move onto the family property. However, Melvin did
not pay any rent to Otis, who agreed to allow his
brother to live in the mutually owned lodge in ex-
change for mortgage payments.
```

If you wanted to highlight Otis' lack of consent, you could rewrite the sentences using *participles (ing* and *ed* verbs used as nouns or adjectives):

```
Allowing Melvin's move into the lodge, Otis never-
theless expected to be consulted in the develop-
ment of the family business.
```

Similarly, you could shift sentence structure into an *appositive* (clarifies and expands meaning of nouns with defining detail, or restates the noun):

> Otis, co-owner and tenant in common, never gave
> consent for the improvements on the family
> property.

A fourth technique for shifting sentence structures is to *coordinate* sentence elements or complete sentences. This coordination creates internal cohesion and equality of ideas:

> Otis visited often, paid half of the property
> taxes, and expected to enjoy his rightful half
> of the commonly held property. [Three coordinate
> verbs set up a cadence and balance that pulls the
> reader into Otis' expectation.]

> Melvin wants a ski resort, but Otis wants a fish-
> ing resort. [Coordinate independent clauses equate
> Melvin's desire for a ski resort, which has al-
> ready been realized, to Otis' desire for a dif-
> ferent kind of resort—making the desires equal
> despite the substantial completion and expense.]

If writers want to hide an element or to give it less prominence, they can *subordinate* it instead of coordinating it (one element in the sentence is dependent and thus carries less weight than the other):

> Although Melvin paid the mortgage and half of the
> taxes, Otis nevertheless paid his share and did
> not require rent from Melvin. [Dependent adverbial
> clause dismisses Melvin.]

> Otis paid his share of taxes, as did Melvin, who
> paid mortgage and taxes but didn't pay rent.
> [Relative clause buries Melvin's contribution.]

Another technique for deliberate sentence structure is to vary sentence lengths, alternating lengths and placing important points in short-short sentences. "Short-short" means really short:

> Otis expected that Melvin, as a co-owner and fam-
> ily member, would consult him about improvements
> and expenditures. He did not. Instead, he took it

for granted that his own desires were those of his
brother, and acted with impunity.

Uncle Otto intended the two brothers to share the
property equally and thus carefully created a tenancy in common for them. Equal here means halves.

In lieu of rent, Melvin paid the mortgage and
arranged for upkeep, including a necessary roof.
Melvin paid half of the taxes. Otis paid half of
the taxes. The brothers shared equally in the necessary payments and balanced out the mortgage
against the rent that Melvin did not have to pay.

Writers can also effectively hammer away at the reader's
subconscious mind through careful use of *repetition*. Words, phrases,
sentences, and even pieces of words can be repeated for this hammering:

Melvin had no authority to create a ski resort,
because Otis never authorized, legally or even by
conversation, the improvements. Melvin had no reason to assume his unauthorized use of the land was
acceptable to either Otis or the law.

Melvin maintained the property by repairing the
roof. But adding a ski resort is not maintenance.
To maintain is to hold the line but not to install
ski lines.

Experimenting with placement, careful writers can manipulate
the emphasis within one sentence:

Melvin moved into the lodge and converted it for
$2.7 million.

For $2.7 million Melvin converted the lodge and
moved into it.

Melvin moved into the lodge and spent $2.7 million
converting it.

Or writers can reinforce the idea in one sentence by beginning the next sentence in a way that repeats the idea:

```
Melvin decided to expand. This expansion necessar-
ily involved spending money. A great deal of money
later, Melvin achieved his goal. This monetary
goal benefited both brothers.
```

Writers rarely create these deliberate sentences in a first draft; they take time and effort. For those documents that need that extra touch or require as much persuasion as possible, however, these techniques justify the expenditure and produce sentences that make the precise points sought by their drafters.

Wanted: Lively Pet or Companion For Elderly Couple.
(Does the couple require a lively companion?)

We want to sell an antique chair and desk.
(Is the desk antique?)

14

BEWARE OF AMBIGUOUS MODIFIERS

Experienced writers move sentence elements from front to back to the middle. That's a sophisticated manipulation to achieve a desired emphasis. Beware, though, moving nouns away from their modifiers. The syntax of English allows descriptive and restrictive words and phrases to modify either one or multiple antecedents, which means that careful writers, each time they draft, need to reflect critically on the options created by their modifier placement. Thus, writers need to be aware that the casual placement of modifiers can destroy intended meaning in contracts, in statutes, and even in argument.

```
You are entitled to transport radioactive material
in Texas and Oklahoma within 100 miles of Dallas.
```

Does the 100-mile restriction apply only to Oklahoma or to both states? Traditional grammarians have recognized this syntactic ambiguity but do not have a rule to prevent the ambiguity. Rather, grammarians can only suggest the author rewrite the string, moving the modifier or repeating it as necessary.

THE DOCTRINE OF THE LAST ANTECEDENT

In 1891 Jabez Sutherland, statute interpreter, created a rule to resolve the problem of interpreting ambiguous modification:

Referential and qualifying phrases, where no contrary intention appears, refer solely to the last antecedent. The last antecedent is the last word, phrase, or clause that can be made an antecedent without impairing the meaning of the sentence. This proviso usually is construed to apply to the provision or clause immediately preceding it. The rule is another aid to discovery of intent or meaning and is not inflexible and uniformly binding. Where the sense of the entire act requires that a qualifying word or phrase apply to several preceding or even succeeding sections, the word or phrase will not be restricted to its immediate antecedent.

Evidence that a qualifying phrase is supposed to apply to all antecedents instead of only to the immediately preceding one may be found in the fact that it is separated from the antecedents by a comma.[1]

Thus Sutherland, given the illustration above, would interpret the 100-mile restriction to apply only to Oklahoma. If the restriction had been preceded by a comma, Southerland would conclude that it referred to both states:

```
You are entitled to transport radioactive material
in Texas and Oklahoma, within 100 miles of Dallas.
```

Writers who are editing their drafts to double-check for ambiguities should be aware that the ambiguous modifier can crop up in a number of syntactical options:

- **a modifier placed *before* two (or more) antecedents:**

```
A police officer by audible or visible means must
identify himself and order the person to stop.
```

[Does the ordering also have to be visible?]

- **a modifier placed *after* two (or more) antecedents:**

```
The petition must be signed by 20 percent of the
qualified voters, residents of the city, who voted
in the last election.
```

---

[1] Jabez Sutherland, Southerland on Statutory Construction §267 (1st ed. 1891).

[Do the people who voted have to be residents?]

- **a modifier placed *after* multiple antecedents:**

    ```
    To qualify for promotion, the police officer must
    be within the weight range for his or her height,
    score 85 on the first test battery, score 90 on
    the special placement battery, and achieve an 85
    percent accuracy score on the shooting range
    within six weeks of the promotion.
    ```

    [What if she was the ideal weight when she applied but is more than that weight within six weeks of the promotion?]

Once attorneys begin to recognize the syntax that creates this ambiguity, they will better be able to avoid it through other syntactic options.

What can be said about the rule's emphasis on the comma to separate out the modifier as one modifying all previous antecedents is disquieting: the comma can always be seen as an indication of multiple antecedents. The absence of the comma, however, can signal either limited modification or sloppy writing. Thus, unless the rule is universally and religiously followed, the rule will always be only a third-tier help for interpretation.

AVOIDING AMBIGUITY

If writers deliberately add a comma to separate the modifier from two or more antecedents, they have a good chance of communicating that it refers to all the antecedents. If they deliberately omit the comma to connect the antecedent to only the closest antecedent, their chances are slim to none that everyone reading will be certain of the intended meaning.

To avoid the ambiguity, writers need to examine carefully each modifier with more than one antecedent. Then they can redraft if there is any chance of misinterpretation. They can (1) repeat the modifier, (2) place the modifier first as a condition precedent and necessary for the following antecedents, or (3) add qualifying words that limit or expand the modifier's application:

1. Repeat the modifier.

```
A. You can transport radioactive material in Texas
   within 100 miles of Dallas and in Oklahoma
   within 100 miles of Dallas.
```

B. We want to sell an <u>antique</u> chair and an <u>antique</u> desk.

C. To qualify for promotion, the police officer must be within the weight range for his or her height <u>within six weeks of the promotion</u>, score 85 on the first test battery, score 90 on the special placement battery, and achieve an 85 percent accuracy score on the shooting range <u>within six weeks of the promotion</u>.

2. Place the modifier first as a condition precedent as necessary.

A. You can transport radioactive material <u>within 100 miles of Dallas in the following states</u>: Texas and Oklahoma.

B. We want to sell <u>two antiques:</u> a desk and a chair.

C. <u>Within six weeks of promotion the police officer must:</u> be within the weight range for his or her height, score 85 on the first test battery, score 90 on the special placement battery, and achieve an 85 percent accuracy score on the shooting range.

3. Add qualifiers that limit or expand the range for the qualifier.

A. You can transport radioactive material <u>only</u> within 100 miles of Dallas in <u>both</u> Texas and Oklahoma.

B. <u>Each</u> of our antiques is for sale: a desk and a chair.

C. To qualify for promotion, a police officer must qualify in <u>all</u> of the following categories within six weeks of promotion: be within the weight range for his or her height, score 85 on the first test battery, score 90 on the special placement battery, and achieve an 85 percent accuracy score on the shooting range.

Admittedly, the solutions above each add additional words to a sentence—but the solutions illustrate why there can never be a pure balance between conciseness and precision in legal writing. Precision always has to outweigh conciseness. Precision is the wedding cake of a marriage between modifiers and their antecedents; conciseness is the cake's icing. In the dilemma of modifier ambiguity, legal writers must sacrifice the icing to make sure there is a celebration at all. Of the above three solutions, the third is the most concise and offers fewest chances of error because it signposts the extended or limited application ("both," "each," "all"). The first solution, repeating modifiers each time, has limited application for especially short modifiers.

THE COURTS' RESPONSES TO THE SUTHERLAND RULE

Attorneys who deliberate and choose syntax carefully will benefit from a review of court decisions based on the ambiguity created by modifiers that have more than one antecedent. Some courts strictly apply the doctrine,[2] some try to stay in the middle of the controversy by looking at both the doctrine and intent,[3] and others choose to ignore the doctrine and favor intent.[4] Some cases have applied contrary theories.[5]

WHY THE DOCTRINE CREATES JUDICIAL PROBLEMS

If the courts strictly applied Sutherland's rule of the last-antecedent comma and used it for both the comma–no-comma distinction, legal writing could be rid of a treacherous ambiguity. But unfortunately, the rule itself calls for interpretation because Sutherland begins with what

---

[2] McCormack Trucking Co. v. United States, 298 F. Supp. 39 (D. N.J. 1969); Elbert, Ltd. v. Gross, 260 P.2d 35 (Cal. 1953); Spears v. State, 412 N.E.2d 81 (Ind. App. 1980); Judson v. Associated Meats & Seafoods, 651 P.2d 222 (Wash. App. 1982); *In re* the Estate of Kurtzman, 396 P.2d 786 (Wash. 1964); *In re* Andy, 302 P.2d 963 (Wash. 1956); Davis v. Gibbs, 236 P.2d 545 (Wash. 1951).
[3] See, e.g., Bass v. United States, 404 U.S. 336 (1971); Gudgeon v. County of Ocean, N.J., 342 A.2d 553 (N.J. 1975); *In re* Renton, 485 P.2d 613 (Wash. 1971); Martin v. Aleinikoff, 389 P.2d 422 (Wash. 1964); Taylor v. Caribou, 67 A. 2 (Me. 1907).
[4] *In re* Newbury Cafe, Inc. (Massachusetts v. Newbury Cafe, Inc.), 841 F.2d 20 (1st Cir. 1988), *cert. granted, judgment vacated, and case remanded,* Massachusetts v. Gray, 489 U.S. 1049 (1989); Sawyer v. State, 382 A.2d 1039 (Me. 1978); Hayes v. State, 247 A.2d 101 (Me. 1968); Stracener v. United Services Automobile Ass'n., 777 S.W.2d 378 (Tex. 1989).
[5] Board of Trustees of Santa Maria Joint Union High Sch. Dist. v. Judge, 123 Cal. Rptr. 830 (Ct. App. 1975); Wholesale Tobacco Dealer's Bur. of S. Cal. v. National Candy & Tobacco Co., 82 P.2d 3 (Cal. 1938); Commonwealth v. Rosenbloom Fin. Corp., 457 Pa. 496 (1974).

seems the fallback rule and concludes with his essential point. He begins with a qualifier, that interpreters should use the doctrine "where no contrary intention appears." Appears where—within the phrase or within legislative intent? If the contrary intent shows up within the sentence itself, then there is no need for the rule. And legislative intent is often in doubt to begin with, so that search is rarely satisfactory. But Sutherland's fifth sentence, "Where the sense of the entire act requires . . . ," implies that the reader has already investigated the phrase within the context of the entire act. The Sutherland rule is a jumble. He probably meant to emphasize intent, and the sense of the act as a whole, over the announced doctrine. It would thus have made more sense for Sutherland to reorganize his sentences to explain his logic sequence:

1. Investigate the act or contract as a whole and judge the ambiguous phrase within its context for consistency and for logic.

2. If investigation does not help, then consider whether applying the doctrine of the last antecedent would go against legislative intent. Stick with legislative intent if it can be determined.

3. If legislative intent is not penetrable, then apply the "doctrine of last antecedent." Although the doctrine is a last-ditch effort to impose logic onto chaos, at least it has its own internal consistency. If everyone followed the doctrine, it would clear up what the document itself and the legislature did not make clear.

Not too surprisingly, courts have had some trouble following and applying Sutherland's rule of construction that was itself written upside down. Courts cannot easily resolve the ambiguities created by misplaced antecedents, either through the rule or by case precedent examining the effects of the rule. It has been applied, misapplied, and dismissed. Thus, legal writers cannot depend on the doctrine to save their documents—they must craft unambiguous phrases to avoid the lottery of misinterpretation.

III
MANIPULATING LEGAL ORGANIZATION
Structure Is Meaning

A major flaw in much legal writing is organization that follows the initial research paper. Expert writers match organization to the document's goal.

15

ORGANIZATION AND THE DEDUCTIVE THRUST

Lawyers are involved in analytical reasoning. Within this conceptual train of thought, they take problems apart and relate their findings back to the initial hypothesis. The more successful writers recognize that the argument or analysis can be most successful when readers can trace this line of reasoning; therefore, careful writers organize the document to reflect the deductive thrust of their argument. They begin with a hypothesis and document the reasoning they underwent to reach a conclusion for that initial hypothesis.

There are three main patterns of organization; much legal writing is *analytical*, in that it is intended to evaluate a point. Accordingly, legal writing will make use of a pattern that parallels deductive reasoning, which moves from a general proof to the axioms or assumptions that it encompasses. Two other major patterns for writing have different goals. The "synthetic" goal speaks from an *inductive* point of view; its thrust is first to compile lists or observations and then to present a conclusion based on that particular evidence. Legal memoranda often follow this pattern, sometimes appropriately, sometimes not. The third pattern, rarely deliberately employed by attorneys, is *rhetorical*. Its development is based on artful, rather than logical, considerations. The author begins and concludes with supporting material, which envelops the message placed in the center of the paragraph or document.

Using a hypothetical state law about a cotenant's contribution for repairs, I have organized one set of facts three ways to allow you to evaluate the effect of organization.

DEDUCTIVE THRUST (ANALYTIC)

Attorneys following a deductive order take the whole and examine the particulars. Beginning with a topic sentence that succinctly states a tentative conclusion (hypothesis), the author builds the paragraphs with supportive facts. In this way, the analytical reasoning is manifested in the style of the paragraph. The examples that develop the paragraph follow the topic sentence and are subordinated to it. The result may be mechanical, but the paragraph or document can be skimmed quickly or studied slowly because the document begins with the main point, as does each of the topic sentences. This clear organization can be outlined as follows:

```
I. First major point's topic sentence
   A. Transition
      1. 2. 3. (etc.) Examples to back up part of
      topic sentence
   B. Transition to next paragraph
      1. 2. 3. (etc.) Examples for second part of
      topic sentence
II. Second major point's topic sentence
```

                . . .

On the sentence level, deduction will consist of complex sentences with both a main clause and one or more subordinate clauses. Deductive sentences reflect dependent relationships, which parallel the paragraph's relationship to its topic sentence. The smallest elements in the document, the words, can also emphasize the subordinate and deductive nature of the message; subordinate signifiers like "*e.g.,*" "*for example,*" and "*for instance*" are consistent with the inherently subordinate nature of the overall design, the paragraph's relationship to the main thesis, and the sentence's relationship to the topic sentence and other sentences within the paragraph.

The paragraph in Figure 4 develops along a subordinate, "deductive" pattern. The initial conclusion ("*She should be reimbursed*") is followed by specific evidence. This organization allows readers to skim the document easily and still understand its main points. When legal writers do not use deductive reasoning, they nevertheless should insert an anticipatory conclusion after stating the issue. Readers therefore know, before digging into the argument, what the writer is about to say.

Upon partition, Delaura Deville should be reimbursed
$18,000 for the repairs she made. She should be re-
imbursed because the general rule is that one
cotenant is entitled to contribution for necessary repairs and improvements when they were
made with the consent of the other cotenants
or when the repairs were necessary for the
preservation of the buildings or land
value. Because she felt responsible,
Delaura, as exclusive tenant, did
make necessary repairs;e.g.,she
corrected foundation problems,a
leaking roof, and inadequate
barn. Although she didn't
ask her cotenant/brother's
permission, she believed
the repairs were neces-
sary. Therefore, after
the land is sold by
partition, she
should receive
reimbursement.

That is why successful legal writers, conscious of their audience's impa-
tience, or curiosity, or hurried reading habits, treat their readers to this
introductory conclusion. They appreciate that legal readers are similar
to readers of other nonfiction documents who want to know what they
are going to read before committing time and effort to the reading. With
the central idea at the beginning of the magazine article, memorandum,
newspaper story, or brief, the readers can then move into the discussion
that follows to learn "why"; with this prior knowledge, they can gain a
better appreciation for the argument that follows.

Unfortunately, legal writers are reluctant to commit themselves to the "what" before they have carefully laid the groundwork with the "why." They offer numerous arguments against this modification:

• Our subject is too serious and too easily misunderstood for a one-sentence or one-paragraph answer.
• We do not want to sound as if there is only one answer to the memorandum question (or one reason for the opinion), and a short answer up front implies just that (i.e., the writers do not want to commit to an early conclusion).
• Readers need to understand the variables and see the historical development.
• Too strong a commitment to one answer defeats the purpose of both a memorandum (to review all options) and an opinion (to explain the legal reasoning that produced the answer).
• No one will ever read my full memorandum again, and I worked hard on those twenty-six pages of writing.
• The conclusion deals with a specific set of facts the reader will not be familiar with yet.
• This modification makes the conclusion repetitive.
• Allowing readers to dictate a prose style to attorneys is ludicrous.

Each of these objections is a valid defense against change, but each ignores the primary rhetorical concern of legal writing: giving the readers the information they need. Legal writers have an obligation, therefore, despite the concerns these objections illustrate, to insert a short introductory conclusion when it is possible. This conclusion helps both writers and readers.

> Question presented: Did our client have a duty to warn his rescuer of the dangers around him?
> Short answer: No, our client's situation meets only two of the four required elements of the "duty-to-warn" test created by the judiciary.

This early deductive conclusion helps writers arrange the discussion of the rules and also helps readers anticipate and follow the discussion. The early conclusion becomes a road map of the terrain to follow. In the above example, for instance, the writer will obviously begin the discussion with a list of the four requirements for the duty-to-warn test. The writer might initially grant that the client's case satisfies two elements of the test. But then the memorandum will investigate the final two elements, explaining how the client's fact situation differs from the remaining two tests that the court requires.

INDUCTIVE THRUST (SYNTHETIC)

Have you ever read the first lines or first paragraphs of a document and wondered what the point was? The author probably allowed the organization to reflect the fact-finding, or conclusion-searching, stage rather than the final conclusion the author reached after examining the evidence.

Induction moves from the particular to the whole, from the details of observation to a general statement about them. An inductive approach builds to a synthesis. These documents or paragraphs march through historical data, piling up details that will later be used as the foundation for a general observation. Legal writers who begin paragraphs with a case name, who next describe the facts of the case, and who only at the end apply the case to a theory or disputed argument are using an inductive method for delivering information. An obvious problem with this technique is that it forces the reader to absorb all the information without a context and then puts the details into a perspective that may—or may not—be similar to the one the reader has had to invent while reading. Frequently this organization suggests that the writer has decided what the point is somewhere in the middle of the paper.

If the author parallels sentences with the aim of induction, the sentences will be coordinate, as opposed to the subordinate sentences of deduction. This coordination reflects the nature of induction, the lists or chronology of details. Sentence structure will probably be simple and compound, rather than complex and dependent. On the word level, the inductive sentence and paragraph will use coordinate signifiers like *i.e.*, *and*, *but*, and *or*. The paragraph in Figure 5, using the same hypothetical law and fact situation as the one in Figure 4, develops through induction.

In this pattern, the author marches us through a chronological statement of the facts and concludes with the general rule of law. Again, the reasoning manifests itself in style: the author is thinking through the situation and asking the readers to think through it along with the author. Notice, though, that the reader is not prepared to judge the facts until the rule is given. And a curious, but frequent, by-product of the inductive thrust is a conclusion that reaches *beyond* the facts given within the paragraph. Why will the court find the repairs necessary? The paragraph gives detail for Delaura's believing they are, but it is a leap to

```
                    Our client,De-
                  laura Deville,oc-
                 cupies a farm given
                to her and her brother
               as cotenants.  She felt
              the house needed repair;
             i.e.,the problem unattend-
            ed would result in decreased
           property  value.  First, the
          shifting  caused the interior
         walls to crack and threaten the
        structural integrity of the house.
       Second, the roof leaked badly. Third,
      the barn's doors were missing, and thus
     the animals were exposed to harsh weather.
    Delaura didn't discuss the repairs with her
   brother, but she realized the necessity and
  spent $18,000.  According to the general rule
 for cotenants,  she will be reimbursed when the
property is sold;her brother did not consent to the
repairs, but the law will find the repairs necessary.
```
Figure 5

assume that the court will agree. Critics label this an inductive leap. If a document requires this inductive approach, legal writers might double-check their conclusions. Unlike the closed circle of a deductive argument, induction may lead a writer into uncharted fields.

ARTFULLY RHETORICAL

Occasionally a legal document is organized with the main point in the middle, of either the entire document or a paragraph. Usually that organization is simply a mistake, a hastily written piece that was perhaps dictated and not reread. If the main point is buried inside a paragraph in a legal document, it is obscured: even careful, perceptive readers frequently miss a buried point. However, outside of legal writing, the deliberate manipulation of sentences to create art has proven effective for writers from Cicero to John Barth. Obviously, the rhetorical thrust is artful, as opposed to problem solving. The intent of the writer is to create an ornate, poetic balance that demonstrates elegance.

In the last rewrite of the hypothetical example (Figure 6), notice the repetition of phrases and the location of the topic sentence. The conclusion rebounds upon the introduction, creating a circle.

Obviously, the rhetorical device works best for literature, although Cicero developed the concept within argument. Its effect is a self-contained, tight structure that parallels its content; unfortunately, few

```
                Delaura Deville

              lives on co-owned

            land and took respon-

          sibility for it. When she

        discovered that the foundation,

      roof, and barn door were deterior-

    ating, she spent $18,000 to preserve

  the property's value.  According to the

general rule, her brother should award her

contribution for this repair upon partition,

  because the repairs were necessary for

    the preservation of the land. Although

      he did not give permission for the

        expenditure, he will benefit from

          the repairs. The award is due

            Delaura because, as a respon-

              sible cotenant, she made

                only necessary repairs.
```

Figure 6

attorneys today have the leisure to construct documents with art as their primary goal and few readers of legal documents patiently explore each paragraph for hidden treasures.

Although attorneys do not always have to organize their material according to a deductive plan, they should be aware of the corollaries and see how the manner of organization can be an expression of the aim. If words and paragraphs work in conjunction with the goal, the writing will have a more consistent effect. Although the writing process becomes highly artificial when it is manipulated in this way, a well-trained mind uses every tool available. If your goal is to persuade, then you will want to make your major points up front and explain them afterward. Double-checking your word choice to make them parallel the aim will help your argument. If your goal is to present information in a memorandum, you can continue to follow the inductive approach of law/cases/application, but it will help to introduce that concluding application first; to begin paragraphs with a list of cases forces readers to accumulate excessive detail before they understand the context.

ORGANIZATIONAL PATTERNS

Attorneys frequently ask for alternatives to their normal organizational patterns. Those standard patterns are chronology for the statement of facts, and IRAC (Issue first, Rule next, Application to facts, and finally Conclusion) for a brief argument and all in-house memoranda. Besides monotony, these patterns create other, equally destructive effects. For instance, a dogged chronology can turn a memorandum into an unapplied history lesson. Chronology is not necessarily the most effective pattern even for a statement of facts, because in complicated cases the facts revolve more around issues of law than time schedules. Chronology can even emphasize the very points you seek to minimize. Similarly, IRAC uses chronology to present the history of the statutes and cases, which leaves the most important material—the conclusion—at the end of the memorandum.

Organization should reflect the writer's purpose and the audience's expectations. Thus, after researching the answer to a legal question, authors should set aside the cases and think through the following kinds of questions:

- What is the most important part of this information?
- What will the reader expect?
- How can I get that information to my reader?

With questions such as these, a writer might, for example, find it important to tell the principal of a school that certain student behavior (causes) needs to result in specific actions by the teachers or board of directors (effects). In another writing scenario, an attorney might need to write a client, describing compliance with a new IRS regulation. Typically this assignment begins with a recitation of the new regulation and concludes with the attorney's recommendations. But that pattern separates the various and probably diverse aspects of the regulation from each recommendation. Asking "What does my client really need to know?" may produce a more useful pattern, perhaps the "oppositional," in which the attorney first lists one area of change and then follows it with what can be done to comply while still maintaining status quo. Or the reader may need to study this new information as steps in a process: to comply with the new tax laws, the client needs to (1), (2), and then (3), etc. As has been noted, how the writer organizes the information depends on the purpose of the document and its audience. If you are unsure of an organizational scheme and want a quick list of options, review the following list:

1. Hierarchical: explaining the most important aspect first and following it with the second tier (etc.) down to the least important, e.g., a brief organized around the opposition's most flagrant violation of the law down to the nit-picking grievances against the opposition's last brief, or a client letter describing must-do steps, ought-to-do steps, and (finally) might-do steps.

2. Examples: extensively illustrating a point. Used as a part of most other organizational patterns, examples can also form the primary pattern, i.e., a basic legal principle illustrated by several cases. Examples can move from *general to specific*, using the underlying legal concept and moving to cases directly on point. Or writers can organize examples from *specific to general*, moving from cases on point to distantly related cases that might not be persuasive but could help round out an argument.

3. Spacial or geographical: describing, for instance, how different areas of the country have interpreted a specific statute, or describing how the elements of a scene are organized: e.g., "Texas courts have not addressed this issue, but most other supreme courts consider proximity to natural waterways as the basis of the argument. Those courts in areas close to large rivers differ significantly from those in areas without major waterways."

4. Steps in a process: outlining the sequence of order, when the reader needs to understand the importance of the parts of a process to understand the whole; e.g., how to set up a limited partnership, or how to convert to a subchapter S corporation.

5. Oppositional: giving a particular argument and then showing what is wrong with it; e.g., an in-house memorandum to a partner listing possible client defenses and their limitations, or a response to a motion that the opposition has just filed.

6. Cause and effect: explaining how one point is the reason for another or how one point is the result or consequence of another. This organization creates strong continuity, especially with the use of definite transitions; e.g., "Why will hiring immigrant labor change an employer's accounting methods? First, the paperwork and hiring procedure . . . . This method creates . . . . Thus the accountants must . . . ."

7. Chronological: telling the story; e.g., a memorandum describing the history of an interpretation, or a brief's traditional statement of facts. Chronology's strength is its narrative; of all organizational patterns, a reader is most likely to remember a story. Its weakness is its inability to emphasize important points or to coordinate/subordinate ideas.

8. Climactic: arranging points in order of ascending importance, from least important to most important (opposite of hierarchical); e.g., to fill a partner in on a court-issued definition, an associate might begin with its more common use and definition and then trace it to a (surprising) current case. Using IRAC, legal writers frequently develop the rules section in this order. Climactic order frequently corresponds with chronological order, but perhaps from a different impetus. The traditional goal of climactic order is to surprise, to startle. In contrast, its use in legal writing ensures that the reader has a complete history in hand to help explain the current court interpretation and the writer's summary of it.

TRANSITIONS

Transitions, those tiny words and almost invisible phrases, link ideas, sentences, and paragraphs. Thus, *a carefully chosen transition* highlights the writer's abstract structural concept, that is, the way the writer believes the ideas connect. *A missing transition* forces the reader to intuit the relationship between parts, which is both frustrating and time consuming. If writers throw in *ill-considered transitions*, the reader not only has to puzzle over the relationship between parts but also must reconstruct the disparate parts into a more logical whole. For these reasons, writers should treat the almost-invisible words carefully. Like the new acrylic glue, transitions hold things together when they are properly applied. But they create chaos if they inadvertently bind. Obviously, the diminutive nature of transitions is deceptive.

Coherence problems develop when writers *omit necessary transitions*. Skilled writers place a transition between case summaries, for instance, to help the reader put the summaries into perspective. For example, two cases may be similar examples of a previously discussed theory and could be joined by one of the "to add" transitions below. These transitions signal a coordinate relationship, hooking together equals and announcing that the paragraphs of material to follow should be read as support for the larger idea. Or, after the general statement of the larger theory, writers may first want to cue the readers that the cases that follow are subordinate to the larger theory and will *illustrate* it. Farther into the memorandum, however, the writer may want to discuss a case that *negates* the earlier ones. Obviously, writers have to think through their use of each case and be able to articulate the relationship between each of the cases they have gathered before they can turn to the list below for help with the specific words they need.

Another major transitional problem is *repetitive transitions*. Using the same phrase to introduce each paragraph, and another repeated phrase to introduce each case example, hurried writers do not take the time to investigate alternatives to the familiar transitions they know will work. As with the necessarily repetitive signals before citations, writers simply and quickly get the job done. The resulting monotony works against their rhetorical goal, but, unfortunately, a realistic solution to these repetitive transitions is not within the time boundaries of most legal writing assignments. Perhaps a simple solution to overused transitions and a quick alternative to the thesaurus is the list offered below.

Warning: The words in each section of this list do not all mean exactly the same thing—they cannot, because each word carries a particular nuance, a shade of definition. The list is meant to trigger your vocabulary memory, not to create one. Therefore, before you insert or substitute these transitions, make sure you understand the subtle difference the substitution creates.

1. To illustrate: for example, for instance, i.e. (coordinate ideas), e.g. (subordinate example), to illustrate, in particular, specifically, to illuminate, to elucidate, to exemplify, to embody, to epitomize.

2. To affirm: actually, certainly, in fact, indeed, surely, undoubtedly, indubitably, unquestionably, positively, precisely, of course, to be sure.

3. To negate: on the contrary, on the other hand, despite, notwithstanding, nonetheless, nevertheless, however, but, conversely.

4. To add: and, also, additionally, another, moreover, or (nor), furthermore, next, again, too, second (etc.), in other words, that is, and then, and besides that, further, likewise, again, even more important.

5. To concede: even though, although, granted that, no doubt, doubtless, certainly, albeit (archaic), whereas, notwithstanding, for all that, although this may be true.

6. To summarize: finally, thus, hence, to sum up, in brief, as has been noted, therefore, in conclusion, accordingly, in short, then, last, to finish, to terminate, consequently, so.

> *"(I)t is usually fiendishly difficult to describe the future course of events in a way that takes account of all the permutations without writing a massive tome that looks like the computer program for a space shot."*
>
> Hollis T. Hurd, <u>Writing for Lawyers</u>

16
ORGANIZATIONAL ADVICE FOR SUCCESSFUL DRAFTING

Drafting is a craft, just as thinking and writing are crafts. For legal drafters, the sophistication necessary for drafting comes from experience, mentors, textbooks, and courses. This critical craft not only *can* be learned; it *must* be learned because failure in drafting is inevitably failure for both the drafters and their clients. Causes of error in drafting can be traced to

- cut-and-paste forms
- office file/personal file
  with dated examples
- complacency
- lack of knowledge or
- deadlines.

TECHNIQUES FOR SUCCESSFUL ORGANIZATION

The draftsman should always clearly and firmly grasp the whole law, deed, or pleading he is to draw, before he commences to draw any part. . . . The best artist (and drafting has been here considered as an art) seldom paints without preliminary sketches.[1]

---

[1] A. J. G. Mackay, *Some General Rules of the Art of Legal Composition*, 32 J. JURISPRUDENCE 169, 179 (1888).

Pre and post outlining

Successful drafters first outline according to client needs that have been established through interviews; then they compare the desired results with established formats. After an initial drafting, they jot down each major heading of the draft, examining their relationships and reorganizing as necessary according to the logic of the document. Next they outline the parts *within* each major heading, again reorganizing those internal parts according to logic.

> In the spatial sequence, the draftsman will find the following rules of thumb helpful, particularly for the main divisions of the instrument:
> (1) General provisions normally come before special provisions.
> (2) More important provisions normally come before less important provisions.
> (3) More frequently used provisions normally come before less frequently used provisions (i.e., the usual should come before the unusual).
> (4) Permanent provisions normally come before temporary provisions.
> (5) Technical "housekeeping" provisions, such as the effective date provisions, normally come at the end.
> In the temporal dimension, the normal ordering of provisions follows the chronology of successive actions or events. This, of course, is one of the most frequently used principles of logical sequence.[2]

Vertical checks

In the earlier writing stage, having divided material into parts, divisions, or sections, the drafter ensures that each separate part is consistent through vertical checks (see Figure 7). The drafter deals with all problems that affect each successive segment.

Horizontal checks

Through horizontal checks (see Figure 7), the drafter checks the definitions one by one throughout the parts, then the cross-references one by

---

[2] REED DICKERSON, THE FUNDAMENTALS OF LEGAL DRAFTING 63–64 (1965).

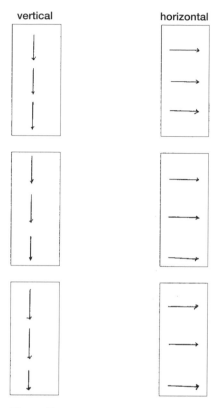

Figure 7

one throughout the parts, and then the citations. The drafter deals with only one problem at a time for the instrument as a whole; e.g., she reviews deadlines and their penalties.

Collaboration

Collaboration is necessary for large, complex jobs. The drafter should not be shy about asking for help in a long or unusual document and not let ego get in the way or worry that everyone else is busy. Any writing can be improved by incorporating an outside reader's response, and drafting of an agreement or a contract requires as much input from different perspectives as possible.

Team cross-checks

Team cross-checks are extended collaboration. Although team *drafting* is usually a disaster, once the initial draft is completed, a team can check and cross-check it. For either individual or team collaboration in final checking, the editorial point of view is freshest the first time the reader goes through the document, so it should be in good order to avoid wasting a precious resource.

Remember, the systematic treatment of form is the means of substantive improvement.

TECHNIQUES FOR SUCCESSFUL EDITING

Through a series of quick steps, legal writers can make even a necessarily long document into one that is accessible to its readers. The first step is to examine the *visual effect* of the pages because long pages and tiny print combine to make reading difficult; even a conscientious client is tempted to skip the reading and instead listen to a summary.

If there is a reason that you do not *want* the parties to read the documents, then retain the traditional, formulaic writing. Otherwise, ask yourself the questions discussed below.

1. Does the introduction provide an *overview* that anticipates the organizational scheme? Traditional legal documents tend to be organized around abstract concepts that are important to the *writer* rather than the *reader*. An effective legal drafter meets consumers' needs when the writer first conceptualizes how the document will be used and then organizes the introduction of the document into a *road map* so that readers can find answers to their most pressing questions quickly and accurately.

> One of the most common mistakes in establishing a logical sequence for the sections of a contract or policy is to start with a series of administrative or "housekeeping" sections. The reader has to wade through this information before getting to the essence of the agreement. A more effective approach is to give readers an overview of the contract or policy at the beginning.[3]

2. Have you concentrated on the *definitions* of words and phrases so that they are internally consistent? Common wisdom is split on when and how to use definitions, but the key to any approach is that it remain consistent. Below are excerpts from several sources on the use of definitions in legal writing.

> Using a definition section allows you to clarify terms and to indicate that a defined term will have the same meaning through-

---

[3] Carl Felsenfeld & Alan Siegel, Writing Contracts in Plain English 97–98 (1981).

out the [statute]. Definitions of words must be clear because your audience will not be able to conform their behavior in the way the legislature intends unless they understand the words.

But insert written definitions sparingly. If you simply use a word in its ordinary meaning, do not define it. To determine whether a definition is needed, consider whether you are adding something or subtracting something from its ordinary meaning or connotation. If you are, define it. Then the courts will follow that definition, even if it is challenged.[4]

As a corollary to this point, eliminate definition sections. . . . Defining terms in context, as opposed to merely presenting a list of defined terms at the beginning of a contract, provides valuable assistance to the reader.[5]

[Y]ou shouldn't define a word in a sense significantly different from the way it is normally understood by the persons to whom the legislation is primarily addressed. This is a fundamental principle of communication and it is one of the shames of the legal profession that draftsmen so flagrantly violate it.

While it may be true, as the philosophers of language like to emphasize, that words have no inherently correct meaning, the communicant who ignores established usage is setting up unnecessary barriers between himself and his audience. This is true even where he gives advance warning, in the form of a specific definition, that he is using his word in a special sense. The lawyer who defines "wheat" as including "rye" is laying a trap not only for his readers but also for himself. This is because of a psychological law that even a legislature is powerless to repeal. Like ghosts returning to a haunted house, established connotations return to haunt the user who attempts to banish them. I have seen many cases where a draftsman, having resorted to this slovenly device, has later forgotten his special definition and reverted unconsciously to the established sense, thereby introducing either an unintended result or an intended result disguised as something else.[6]

---

4 Mary B. Ray & Barbara J. Cox, Beyond the Basics 29 (1991).
5 Felsenfeld & Siegel, *supra* note 3, at 98.
6 Reed Dickerson, *How to Write a Law*, 31 Notre Dame L. Rev. 14, 25–26 (1955).

A definition should say a word either "means" or "includes" the remainder of the words used in the definition. If the definition is intended to be exhaustive and exclude everything not included in the definition, use "means." If the definition is intended to be only partial and permit the word to be applied to things included in the definition, use "includes." Do not say "includes but is not limited to." The words "but is not limited to" are redundant.[7]

3. Can the reader quickly find the way through the document by reading *headings and subheadings*? Are the headings clearly delineated by location or typeface?

4. Is the *paragraph length* manageable? How long is too long? Can more than one paragraph fit logically beneath the numbered or captioned introduction?

5. Will *tabulation* help break up the necessarily dense paragraphs? If so, you should review the rules on tabulation.

6. WHY DO SOME DRAFTERS USE ALL THOSE *CAPITAL LETTERS*? READING SENTENCES LIKE THIS COULD DRIVE A NORMALLY SEDATE PERSON WILD. Unless mandated otherwise, you should reserve capital letters for the beginnings of sentences and proper nouns.

7. Are the *sentence lengths* manageable? One thought = one sentence? Typical contract sentences contain so many qualifiers and embedded clauses that readers must expend mental energy to untangle them before they can process the messages within the sentence.

8. Are *qualifying phrases close to their antecedents*? Most ambiguity that reaches litigation begins with agreements created by phrases thrown into sentences without regard to the sentence's syntactical meaning.

9. Can you "say less" and still say the same thing? In the attempt to be precise, are you instead *redundant*?

> *Before:* The Board may appoint, discharge at pleasure, and fix the compensation of the secretary and such clerical force as from time to time in its judgment may be necessary in the administration of this subtitle if it has funds available for the payment of such persons . . . . (Md. Ann. Code art. 56, §466(b) (1988).)

---

[7] ROBERT MARTINEAU, DRAFTING LEGISLATION AND RULES IN PLAIN ENGLISH 106–107 (1991).

After: The Board may employ a staff in accordance with the state budget. (Md. Bus. Occ. & Prof. Code Ann. §3.204(d) (1989) as revised by the Division of Statutory Revision, Division of Legislative Reference, Maryland General Assembly.)[8]

10. Have you eliminated *arcane expressions* (jargon versus terms of art)?

Whether sound, enforceable contracts can be written without the traditional legalistic style and vocabulary is the key issue in the plain English movement.[9]

11. Have you *punctuated* to avoid ambiguity? Punctuation creates meaning. If you are unsure of the basic rules for punctuating or want to review options, choose one style manual and use it consistently.

CONCLUSION

Drafting a legal document takes time, patience, experience, and skill. Efficient drafters practice the above steps during editing often enough that the process eventually moves faster, requires less patience, and reflects more experience and skill. But it is still hard work.

Some drafters are disappointed that there's little room for creativity in drafting. I can respond, "Be happy you're not required to be creative too." The goal of a creative writer is to produce something so interesting that it can compete with Monday-night football. Drafting simply has to pass the scrutiny of today's courts and future researchers.

---

[8] JANICE REDISH, HOW TO WRITE REGULATIONS (AND OTHER LEGAL DOCUMENTS) IN CLEAR ENGLISH 9 (1983).
[9] FELSENFELD AND SIEGEL, *supra* note 34, at iv.

17

QUICK TRICKS FOR ORGANIZATION

Suppose you have a rough draft but suddenly need to send the completed document off: I am not describing a mythical hypothetical situation but rather a weekly reality. Research can consume so much time that there is little left to organize the results. The following techniques are meant not to replace thoughtful development but rather to aid your audience to understand the material as much as possible when careful organization must be sacrificed to the necessity of speed.

INITIAL SETUP

Skim through the research and decide what the audience needs to know about your conclusion. Although you may not have time to reorganize your whole draft to show how you reached that conclusion, you can nevertheless add that necessary *conclusion* about the results of your research at the beginning of your draft, plus a *road map* that anticipates the research path. This initial setup will guide readers through even the most jumbled draft material.

MARGINAL NOTATIONS

If you discover that you have additional time after adding the initial setup paragraph, you can skim each subsequent paragraph in the draft, noting in the margins only a word or two to describe the paragraph's contents. These can be judged quickly, as if they were an outline. You can then piece similar material together from the margin outline so that each section contains its own internal logic, even if there is no time to reorder those lumps into a larger coherence. You can return to the initial setup paragraph and add an outline of these sections. If there is still time, you should reorder the large lumps into a more coherent order. Either way, the initial setup must be changed to reflect any new ordering.

TOPIC SENTENCES

Topic sentences function as major highway signs to help travelers understand which branch of the discussion's highway they are getting ready to enter. Devise strong topic sentences that carry the discussion. Topic sentences should not obscure your message with summaries of case holdings. Your readers should be able to understand from that paragraph's topic sentence *why* they are going to read the details of the examined case, what legal idea that case stands for.

Organization is order. Thus, an initial setup paragraph that announces three prongs should have a topic sentence that follows the announced order of those three prongs.

HEADINGS AND SUBHEADINGS

If time allows the addition of even more glaring clues to guide organization, you can divide major bulks of paragraphs with headings and subheadings that highlight the initial setup.

If you are an organized draft writer, you may already have the headings written before you add detailed paragraphs. In that case, you can return to the introduction and simply add a setup that announces your established headings. Whether you jot randomly or outline with headings first, these organizational tricks can help even antagonistic readers appreciate the ease of reading brightly sign-posted documents.

No one has ever complained that a document was too easy to follow. As you can see below, organizing your draft can be done quickly—and your readers will thank you for it!

TRICKS FOR DEADLINE ORGANIZING

At 5:30 P.M. an attorney is just finishing a research task when someone calls, insisting the results need to be on the opposing counsel's desk the next morning at 7:00. The last mail courier leaves at 6:30 P.M., and what the writer has in the computer so far is raw notes with no discernible organization or conclusion.

This is not an unlikely scenario.

Below is an emergency plan that will allow you to send understandable, if not polished, material:

5:30

1. Run a spell-check while you decide what you've learned from the research.

5:35

2. At the top of your document, insert that conclusion. At the bottom of the document, apply that overall conclusion to your facts.

5:40

3. Ask: What does this audience really need to know quickly at 7 A.M.? Make sure the answer is in your first paragraph.

5:45

4. Now, run off a rough draft of the whole document and skim through it, quickly summarizing each paragraph with a word or two in the margin.

5:55

5. On a separate sheet of paper, copy the list of summaries from your margins.

6:00

6. Group similar ideas into lumps: cases with facts on point, for instance; public policy; all the paragraphs about the same case. Cut and paste these lumps together.

6:10

7. Move the grouped paragraphs into some order that will help the readers. This step may be the most difficult: if you are boggled, leave the paragraphs in random order and move on.

6:15

8. Return to your introductory paragraph, where you have already told the reader the most important part of the document. Now indicate to the readers what material will follow and in what order. This information is your setup. It would be especially useful if the material were in a logical order, but even if it is not, the readers can still be introduced to the overall organization and learn where to find the part they need the most.

6:20

9. Time left over? Add headings to signal the division between major ideas.

6:25

10. One more spell-check, sign, and send.

IV
MANIPULATING WORDS
Bigger Isn't Better

18
JARGON
Manure, Margarine, and Moderation

Jargon is technical shorthand. It is useful—as long as legal writers limit it to its intended audience. But that audience frequently complains that the law they must read is unintelligible. Perhaps if experienced writers distinguish between two types of jargon, they can decide which are appropriate words and which extend beyond the boundaries of their audience's understanding or forbearance.

One type of jargon is "terms of art." These words are necessary shorthand used by the initiated, those people who have attended law school or studied the legal precedent of the word and the larger concept it symbolizes. Legal writers, for instance, addressing a court about a jurisdiction problem must be able to use "quasi in rem" if necessary; to eliminate this term of art would require writers to define and repeat formulas for words that both writers and readers have in common. It is obvious that terms of art serve a useful function: if a writer employs them to best advantage, they convey both an instant message and a recognition of the intended audience. These are not words that should be dropped simply because a lay audience does not recognize them.

You might question the necessity of terms of art, of course, especially when you notice that they litter your pages more frequently than nontechnical words, but attorneys should not berate themselves for using these terms when they are necessary. Term-of-art jargon is jargon only to an outside audience. To an intended audience, it conveys a message succinctly.

I once read an art critic's review of two painters. He said that one made liberal use of his paints, like "a farmer spreading barnyard manure." The other painter hoarded his paints like "wartime margarine." That is an applicable analogy for a variety of writing problems: from slang to "which's," metaphors to jargon. Some legal writers overuse jargon; because it is readily at hand, they apply it in thick layers without considering the effect the combination of terms of art and unnecessary jargon can have on readers. Not even a legally trained audience wants to trudge through unnecessary jargon.

This second type of jargon is jargon that can be eliminated either entirely or in part. Some of the words (underlined) can be eliminated entirely:

```
the aforesaid plaintiff
enclosed herein [and] herewith
null and void
it is hereby ordered
said defendant
Juicy Fruit, hereinafter the seller (and here-
    inafter cited as)
save and except
witnesseth [A pause between identification in a
    contract and the details—adds nothing and can be
    deleted.]
deem and consider
covenant and agreement
give, devise, and bequeath ["Bequeath" may now
    govern real property as well as personal.]
in truth and in fact ["Truth" is distinguished
    from fiction or error, and the purpose of the
    court will be to prove these statements, so
    the fact will determine the actual occurrence
    anyway.]
be it remembered
know all men by these presents
whereas [to introduce recitals, e.g., "Whereas, no
    one reads this part anyway . . ."]
in lieu, in place, instead of, and in substitution
    for
to have and to hold [old common-law terms for con-
    veyance]
```

last will and testament [A will now relates to
both real and personal property, unlike the situation in earlier English law which separated
them. Many attorneys express serious discomfort
changing the names of legal documents, so I
doubt this redundancy will ever die.]

annul and set aside [An imbalance of phraseology.
"Annul" is one option of setting aside and would
mean the same thing without the unnecessary
words. However, "to set aside" can mean a variety of things: to reverse, vacate, cancel, annul, or review. So if you are describing the action of a court, you might qualify how the court
set aside the ruling by adding, for example,
that the court set aside the opinion for review.
Another option might be that an appellate court
will set aside its decision by reversing it or
canceling it.]

Other barnyard jargon has evolved from the Old English/Latin/
French overlay of important legal terminology. Many of them are today
merely repetitious:

acknowledge and confess
act and deed
authorize and empower
covenant and surmise
due and payable
each and all
fit and proper
for and in consideration of
force and effect
fraud and deceit
give and grant
give, devise, and bequeath
keep and maintain
lot, tract, or parcel of land
modified or changed
null and void
null and void and of no force or effect
ordered, adjudged, and decreed
truth and veracity

A second group of jargon words may not be synonymous, but they need to be reconsidered. The coupled words below are not parallel or equal, in spite of the conjunction that signals they will be. For example, *fraud and deceit* is frequently written as a phrase, joined by the conjunction "and." But fraud is a cause of action that contains the element of deceit, along with other elements (the purpose of inducing another to part with a valuable thing or legal right). If you have committed fraud, you have deceived; that is a conditional relationship rather than a conjunctive one. Deceit is merely one aspect of fraud. While an element of fraud, deceit is also an element of other causes of action. Deceit is also deceptive misrepresentation that does not lead to any cause of action. Parents lying to their children about Santa Claus deceive them, but they are not guilty of breaking any law. If you have *defrauded* someone, you have necessarily deceived her. But if you have *deceived* someone, you have not necessarily defrauded her. The phrase is used incorrectly if the two words are joined by a conjunction that indicates that the words are equals.

Another coupled phrase, *acknowledge and confess*, contains an internal redundancy. To acknowledge is defined as "to own, avow, or admit; to confess; to recognize one's acts and assume responsibility." So the definition contains "confess." Acknowledge is the larger entity, and confession is one of the aspects of it. They are not parallel and equal.

Due and payable has the same problem; both mean that justice or the law requires something owed, payable. In this case, though, *payable* may signify an obligation to pay at once, so it subsumes *due* within this phrase and becomes redundant. Play it safe and drop one of the terms; keep the one that actually applies.

Some attorneys routinely include jargon in client letters to make the document "look legal" and to justify the bill that will follow. That practice is using jargon for a purpose, at least. And others include the terms of art to "muddy up" the issue—if they summarize a legal situation too simply, clients may later take legal action because they feel they were misled by the easy-reading summary. That's another deliberate use of jargon—whether the audience accepts it is a matter of consequence and conscience.

Most jargon used for the lay audience, however, is probably the result of writers' lack of audience awareness coupled with those notorious time constraints. It is neither a deliberate shoveling of manure nor an attempt to avoid wartime margarine.

I would like to counsel moderation in jargon: if you write to a legal audience, use necessary terms of art but consciously avoid pretentious and distracting phrases. If you write to a mixed audience, you need to adjust to the variety of readers' expectations. That is easier said than done, unfortunately, like most advice about writing.

Many firms repeatedly draw up similar documents for a lay audience (wills, divorce agreements, lease agreements, agreements of purchase and sale, warranty deeds, deeds of trust). It makes sense to have someone in the office take the time to write and file a sample client letter that could be attached when the document is sent. The sample would be written by someone with experience in that area of the law. This cover letter would explain the traditional aspects of the document and leave places for the writer to highlight any unusual aspect of the document. Naturally, individual writers would adjust the detail to each client's case. Once the firm has these sample client letters on file, clients would not have to be billed for all the extra time to carefully reword each document.

These jargon-free form letters might even include a disclaimer: "The information in this letter is intended to generally summarize the material of the enclosed document. It is not intended as a substitute for and does not fully reflect the entire document. We encourage you to read the enclosed document carefully and call us if you have any questions."

Assuming the accompanying document (in-house memorandum, brief, formal agreement) avoids at least the barnyard variety of jargon, you would then send both the cover letter and the legal document to the client.

19

BOILERPLATE
Empty Formalisms

Attorneys worried about a court's response to anything new use boilerplate because they assume the court accepts it. Judges skim it, but accepting it is something else. Indeed, Judge Lynn Hughes, moving from state to federal court, made *Houston Chronicle* headlines in 1986: "Ban the Bull: Judge shows no mercy to lawyer's lingo." Seems he lost his patience while reading yet another brief full of "excessive capitalization, empty formalisms, obscure abstractions and other conceptual and grammatical imbecilities."[1] Form pleadings, for example, usually repeat the complete title of the pleading in the first paragraph.

```
Plaintiffs' Reply to Defendant's Brief in Opposi-
tion to Smith's Motion for Summary Judgment
    Plaintiffs, John T. Smith et al. (hereinafter
"Smith"), file this Brief in Reply to McElroy Cor-
poration's (hereinafter "McElroy") Response to
Smith's Counter-Motion for Summary Judgment and in
Support of Plaintiffs' Counter-Motion for Partial
Summary Judgment and would respectfully show the
Court the following: . . .
```

▬▬▬

[1] Of that list, only excessive capitalization is easy to correct. For rules on capitalization, see TEXAS LAW REVIEW MANUAL ON STYLE ch. 1 (7th ed. 1992).

Experienced writers can avoid that wasted space with only one sentence:

```
Plaintiffs, John T. Smith et al., support their
reply with the following: . . .
```

Inexperienced writers fear that avoiding boilerplate totally will (1) waste a client's money while the attorneys rewrite the form books, (2) risk a client's case with innovative language, or worse, (3) make the court suspicious by paraphrasing instead of quoting the exact language of cases and statutes.

Most attorneys assume the form books "work." The forms have survived legal challenges and probably will not call attention to themselves. They work. Legal secretaries, paralegals, and new associates can fill in the blanks. Unfortunately, judges become so familiar with the stock phrases of boilerplate that they skip right over them, occasionally to the detriment of an important fact or procedural issue. The judge cannot anticipate the occasion when token phraseology creates meaning.

In addition to form books, attorneys necessarily rely on precedent and statutes to build their cases. The result is long, poorly written judicial paragraphs that are lifted directly into the briefs, either blocked and single-spaced or altered ever so lightly and included in a never-ending text of proof for the almost-forgotten rule. Only experienced attorneys dare paraphrase statutes, and few deviate from total reliance on long, blocked quotations. And whom are the attorneys quoting? Right—legislators and judges.

What has evolved here is a cycle of discontent. Judges do not want to read attorneys' formulaic writings, but the attorneys are no happier with the opinions and forms they feel they are required to use. Judges have excellent reason to complain about empty forms and unnecessary repetition. And attorneys have excellent reason to complain about both the similar language in opinions and the lack of available, simplified form books.

Until one of these groups commits itself to radical and consistent change, the cycle will continue. Let's examine the positive options for attorneys:

- The State Bar of Texas should be encouraged to continue revising its form books.
- Individually or collectively, attorneys can approach the authors of popular form books, requesting that they speed up the revisions of outdated language.

- Law firms can assign their attorneys cleanup duty for frequently used forms. Although some of the forms' language is the result of hard-fought court cases, many of the stock phrases in forms can be deleted or replaced without changing the meaning of the sentence: "To the Honorable Judge *of Said Court*." If firms accept the form modification as a long-term project that will benefit the future of the firm, an attorney could edit, one document at a time, the most-used forms. The cost would be absorbed by the firm and everyone would benefit; indeed, billing time might even be saved because new associates could understand what they are doing a little better and faster.
- Attorneys, with more control over their briefs than over their pleadings, can eliminate from the body of the brief obvious jargon and old formalities: "respectfully submit," "time is of the essence," "be it remembered," "whereas," "just and reasonable," "to wit."

The courts can also help break the cycle of bad writing:

- Judges can join the State Bar in its attempts to provide adequate form books that reflect the best options for legal writers.
- Judges can take a firm stand against legalism and offer style sheets of positive examples. For example, Federal Judge Tom Gee gives his clerks a two-page summary of stylistic errors he wants them to avoid.
- Judges can discourage the inclusion of long, single-spaced quotations by asking their clerks to insist these long passages be attached in an appendix.
- Judges can hold mini-classes, helping attorneys understand how to incorporate precedent and statutes without quoting long blocks of rhetoric.
- In class or specially arranged conferences, judges and attorneys could share their impressions about legal writing; myths would give way to reality, and both groups would benefit from the exchange.
- In their own writing, judges can avoid long quotations and court boilerplate. Within each court, judges can constantly remind each other of the need for stark, informative writing. And, of course, they can fight the urge to publish every opinion.

> *"Anyone who has ever written anything—especially recently—has faced the problem of his/hermaphrodism . . . . To be fair, you don't want to favor one sex over the other. To solve this problem of fairness, we seem to have developed a new gender, one that shares maleness and femaleness simultaneously, equally, and therefore fairly. We have, in short, created—out of nowhere—a his/hermaphrodite."*
>
> *(C. Edward Good, <u>Mightier than the Sword</u>)*

20

GENDER-NEUTRAL LANGUAGE

SALUTATIONS

Most attorneys worry about how to address a letter when the only name they know is the name of the office or agency they are addressing. They are uncomfortable with the traditional salutations "Dear Sir" and "Dear Gentlemen" and worry that "Dear Ladies and Gentlemen" sounds like the beginning of a speech.

One solution for attorneys who frequently write to unknown representatives of agencies or corporations might be to address their correspondence to the *office*: "Dear Examiner" (Securities and Exchange Commission, Internal Revenue Service), "Dear Counsel" (attorney general's office, legal staff of a corporation), "Dear Board Member" (commissioners, local governing boards). Depending on the writer's perception of me, I receive mail addressed "Dear Professor," "Dear Investor," and even "Dear Cable Subscriber." Rather than being offended by this impersonal salutation, I find that the salutation gives me an early cue about the letter's content.

However, not every writer is comfortable beginning with "Dear Banker." For some, the substitution of an office name for the traditional "Dear Sir" or "Dear Ladies and Gentlemen" may create more problems than it solves because it focuses too quickly on the nonfamiliar and impersonal relationships of strangers. Even worse is "To Whom It May Concern." I am always reminded of a note floating ashore in a bottle: "Hey you out there," the salutation calls, "see if my message affects you." If "Dear Banker" is too impersonal and "Dear Deadbeat Debtor" too specific, you may want to pick up the telephone and ask whom you will be addressing in the letter.

Occasionally, you can learn the addressee's initials, but they do not help you determine her or his sex. In those cases, you can always address the letter to the full name: "Dear M. A. Johnson" or "Dear W. S. Southerland."

That the question of salutations remains under debate reveals an evolving society. Your daily decision about salutations will create, in the long run, part of the answer to the problem of sexist language.

SHE/HE/THEY/IT

Although everyone has an opinion, few people agree on the solution to the third-person singular pronoun confusion. The majority of practitioners who graduated in the early 1980s or earlier accept the traditional approach—using *he* to include *she*. They reject the *he/she* and *s/he* as intrusive, bulky, unnecessary, and even radical. Against that wall of resistance, few established practitioners are willing to attempt stylistic and social modification. Academic legal writers, on the other hand, have adopted a variety of approaches in an effort to avoid pronoun difficulties.

According to traditional drafters and legal historians, the legal world is not an appropriate arena for social statements. In other words, since legal writers are usually already involved in a substantive battle, they don't want to complicate the original fight with a side issue that will not help their side and may instead damage it.

Unlike their more conservative counterparts, though, more liberal authorities acknowledge the need for social change—especially in the legal arena. Where else can change take place, they reason, if not in the language of our legal system that creates rules for other public arenas?

UNDERSTANDING YOUR "PARTNER"

Legal writing should deliver information, persuade, establish authority, console, or cajole. These purposes require a partnership between reader and author repeatedly defined by the writer's choice of written words. This relationship obviously depends on language. But the English language does not have a common-gender pronoun for the third-person singular. *It* signifies an inanimate, genderless object and can be useful if the legal actors are corporations. Unfortunately, writers chance creating confusion if they use multiple *it*s within the sentence as both pronouns and expletives (when *it* functions as an anticipatory subject or object). Only our third-person plural, *they*, is unambiguous because it is neutral and does indeed subsume both male and female.

Many readers are disturbed or offended by the use of *he* as a generic term that represents both males and females. Because of their vocal disapproval, they have given today's legal writers notice: insensitivity to this linguistic change reflects insensitivity to important social changes.

SENSITIVITY

By the time law students become drafters of statutes and contracts, they have been shaped by the language they have read. Unfortunately, law students today are being molded by casebooks still peopled with only males—it is a rare opinion that uses *she* as a generic term for a person. Unless a plaintiff or defendant is female, students will not find a reference to the other half of society. Meanwhile, the lively debate continues over whether language conditions society or whether it reflects society.

This dilemma is not easily resolved. If for no other reason, attorneys *should* become involved in the question of nonsexist language because sexist language is often imprecise and excludes much of its audience. *He* does not always mean only *he*, so the word is ambiguous. Manipulating pronouns may have the pleasant side effect of cleaning up verbiage, making prose cleaner, crisper, and quicker ("A landlord needs legal protection if . . ."). So if it is within the scope of their documents, legal writers should insist on nonsexist language. A dash of common sense will keep them from sacrificing their clients just to make a gratuitous social statement—imagine a court's response to a brief replete with *he/she* or one that corrects a statute with [*s*] before any *he* in the statute. One legal writer amazed his audience with an unparalleled—and embarrassing—series of well-intended slashes: s/he/it.

Until the world has changed into a better place, or until readers decide *he* is an inclusive term, or until someone invents an acceptable substitute, cautious writers will have to minimize the dilemma. Some issue-avoiding options are discussed below.

VARIATIONS

1. Drop the pronoun. "An owner may be the last to know that *his* tenant has moved" can be rewritten as "An owner may be the last to know *a* tenant has moved." If this omission creates internal ambiguity, use a different option.

2. Use the third-person plural where possible. "A party who intends to raise an issue concerning the law of a foreign country should give notice in *his* pleadings or other reasonable written notice" can be rewritten as "*Parties* who intend to raise an issue concerning the law of a foreign country shall give notice in *their* pleadings or other reasonable written notice."

Admittedly, not all sentences can be rewritten into the plural and still make sense. If the plural creates additional ambiguity or contradicts the language of a statute being analyzed, try another of the options.

3. Remember the first and second persons. In letters and informal memoranda, *I*, *me*, *we*, *our*, *you*, and *your* can add life and a degree of intimacy. *We* and *our* also enliven briefs.

4. Add female terms occasionally, when it is important to emphasize the possibility of either gender. *She or he* can be effective, if you do not have to repeat it consistently and if the rest of the sentence is simple enough to support the bulk. Admittedly, a statute revised in that manner could double in length—making the cure as bad as the initial problem. Most readers find the slashes and parentheses in *he/she*, *he (or she)*, and *s/he* distracting. Ironically, most of these forms place the male in the first position, as if the female is included as a trendy afterthought.

If you are illustrating through example, vary the sex of the characters. Just make sure that you do not stereotype the women into "female" occupations.

5. Define *he* as a generic word, which acknowledges traditional usage. Defining *he* is an admission of both the problem and the lack of a better solution. Contracts and wills contain formalized sections for definitions; if each *he* is intended to include both sexes, define it as such at the beginning or in a footnote. However, wills and contracts are client-specific, so many of the pronouns should reflect your fact situation. Briefs can include the generic definition within a footnote. Federal statutes are governed by 1 U.S.C. § 1 (1982): "words importing the masculine gender include the feminine as well. . . ." Texas statute attempts to solve the problem with a similar disclaimer: "The masculine gender includes the feminine and neuter genders."[1]

6. Use *she* and *he* as generics. Alternate using *she* and *he* in different sections or chapters.

---

[1]TEX. GOV'T. CODE ANN. § 312.003(e) (Vernon 1988).

PRAGMATICS OF MODERATION

Language will not change unless the change is logical. Attempts to invent a new third-person pronoun have failed. Perhaps if Madonna and Michael Jackson incorporated a new term into their rock lyrics, the English-speaking world would change overnight. But even in that farfetched scenario, the newly coined word would have to be compatible with our sense of what a pronoun sounds like ("tey," "whe"). More likely, our speech habits will blend into acceptable prose, so that "Everyone must represent their client to the best of their abilities" will be understood to refer to the singular, despite the plural pronoun. Unfortunately, that language will be ambiguous—just without the sexist connotation.

GENDER-SPECIFIC NOUNS

Nouns, in contrast to pronouns, have more easily changed as our society has changed. Examples are *aviator*, now an inclusive term that has replaced *aviatrix*, and *freshman*, a term that now includes both sexes. Society enlarges the concept behind the term to include women, and the noun then refers to both sexes.

Attorney (agent authorized to act for someone) and *lawyer* (a person learned and licensed to practice the law) both are gender-neutral, but *esquire* has only gradually become so. Originally an English title "of dignity next above gentleman," a candidate for knighthood, or an escort, Americans use it as a title after the name of an attorney (male or, more recently, female). The legal title that continues to create confusion is *draftsman*. Because it contains *man*, like *fireman*, *postman*, *chairman*, and *policeman*, it signals a masculine construction. Now terms like *firefighter*, *postal clerk* or *mail carrier*, and *police officer* substitute easily and have been widely accepted; this text substitutes *drafter* for *draftsman*.

A published in-house squabble in the Texas Court of Criminal Appeals about the use of "prosecutrix" illuminates the discomfort and confusion created by sex-based words.[2] In this case, the court, sitting en banc, used the word "prosecutrix" to describe the victim of a sexual assault. The legal question before Judge John Onion's court was whether the victim's previous sexual experience should have been introduced at

---

[2] Allen v. State, 700 S.W.2d 924 (Tex. Crim. App. 1985).

trial. But, after concurring with a seventeen-page answer to the legal question, Judge Chuck Miller and Judge Marvin Teague issued separate opinions, not about the legal issue but about the language contained in the opinion describing the chief complainant. Throughout the opinion, she is the "prosecutrix."

Judge Miller takes issue with "prosecutrix" instead of "victim." Quoting *Black's Law Dictionary*, he defined "prosecutrix" as "a female prosecutor" and distinguishes that role from that of a victim called on to present evidence in her own case. Judge Miller objects to the term's use for three reasons: the use is inconsistent with the definitions in source materials, the term is "blatantly sexist," and the use of "prosecutrix" rather than "victim" is prejudicial to the victim because it implies that there is no *victim* in a sexual-assault case. He concludes, "In sum, the term 'prosecutrix' should be relegated to the attic trunk, along with corsets and pantaloons, and the term 'victim' placed in its stead." [3]

Judge Teague's five-and-a-half-page response to Judge Miller begins rather lightly: "My, oh, my, how Judge Miller does fulminate over Presiding Judge Onion's use in his majority opinion of the age-old legal word 'prosecutrix.'" [4] Backtracking, he sets the stage for his rebuttal by agreeing with the legal conclusion to the original opinion. He follows this token nod to the purpose of the opinion with a quotation from Mary Claire-Van Leunen on the stylistic problems feminists face by not using *he* generally.

Reaching beyond *Black's Law Dictionary* for his authority, Judge Teague quotes both *Webster's Third New International Dictionary of the English Language* and the *Oxford English Dictionary* (*OED*) to show that "prosecutrix" includes the feminine Latin ending for "agent nouns" (instead of "-or" for masculine or generic). The agent noun in this case derives from the verb "prosecute." One who prosecutes, who is a witness for the prosecution, is a "prosecutor." Now, although "prosecutor" is masculine, Judge Teague reasons, it is not "necessarily so, since it also serves a generic function; the content will determine in which sense the word is to be understood." [5] The judge concludes that the term does encompass the intended definition of the complainant (a female) in a criminal prosecution.

---

[3] *Id.* at 936.
[4] *Id.* at 932.
[5] *Id.* at 934.

Although "prosecutrix" may have more meanings than merely "complaining witness" or "complainant," the victim of sexual assault has been called "the prosecutrix" by the court for many years, and "such usage has always been understandable by most rational persons . . . if she has, indeed, appeared as the chief witness for the State."[6] It always has been; ergo, it is. But even longtime readers of criminal court opinions may wonder why the term is usually reserved for sexual-assault cases.

Judge Teague informs us that "prosecutrix" is inherently sexist in the sense that it implies a difference in treatment or favor on a basis other than individual merit (*Oxford English Dictionary*). Justice Teague concludes by insisting that he "should like to go on the record that I cannot find anywhere that makes it readily and immediately apparent in the etymology of the words 'prosecutrix' or 'prosecutor' that might suggest that any pejorative connotation should be, or ever was, attached to these words."[7]

It is a shame we cannot poll juries to find out if they are equally affected by the terms *victim* and *prosecutrix*. I am not. I doubt the young assaulted woman and her attorney are. The term that refers to the "victim" is subtly undermined by its connotative associations with the attacker. Attorneys using the opinion as precedent may intellectually recognize its definition, but *intuitively* they will respond to its connotations. The specialized sense of "prosecutrix" strongly suggests the aggressor, the one attacking. Maybe Judge Teague and those with *OEDs* on their desktops would generously grant the technical definition of the term without allowing its overtones to affect them. Unfortunately, the use of "prosecutor" or "prosecutrix" muddles the victim and attacker roles. To testify for the prosecution does not turn the victim into the original attacker. But "prosecutrix" and "prosecutor" suggest aggression. Perhaps in most criminal cases the connotations attached to the victim do not affect the outcome of the case. But they certainly do in a sexual-assault case. To believe otherwise is either deliberately obfuscating or naive. In the majority of other court opinions, "complainant" and "victim" have replaced "prosecutor." So should they in sexual-assault cases.

---

[6] *Id.* at 933.
[7] *Id.* at 935.

Ernest Hemingway mirrored all of us when he admitted to rewriting the end to A Farewell to Arms thirty-nine times because he had trouble "getting the words right."[1]

21
THAT'S NOT WHAT I MEANT

Can you think of one word that has absolute meaning?

Law is a process of interpreting language; language consists of our words and their relative positions in a sentence, paragraph, and document. Language is not a constant a writer can depend on, whether the subject is law or literature-and-life.

Most legal drafters agree that words are finally indefinable, that it is impossible to constrict and restrict words enough that each reader can automatically understand the intended "meaning." Only the unusually naive insist they do not interpret as they listen and read. And lawyers cannot afford that naiveté. Nevertheless, inexperienced legal readers are highly susceptible to believing that the word and thing are the same:

> . . . they often slip just one peg down into the deeply-rooted notion that the word inevitably and unalterably belongs to a particular thing or person. A name is like a label chained around the object of God's order, which nobody must presume to detach. "And whatsoever Adam called every living creature, that was the name thereof." Lawyers and judges are highly sus-

---

[1] WRITERS AT WORK: THE *PARIS REVIEW* INTERVIEWS 222 (George Plimpton ed., 2d ser. 1963).

ceptible to this notion of an indissoluble link between the word and the thing.[2]

Only by examining legal prose can we confront inherent ambiguities. But unless we resort to pictures (which have their own sets of problems), we must work with our words: twist them, cajole them, inflate them, deflate them, encourage them, delete them.

The frenzy within the legal profession over the nomination of Robert Bork to the Supreme Court may have surprised the rest of the nation, but it was representative of the large-scale board of opinions across which attorneys are frequently aligning themselves on the question of "intent." Questions of intent invariably arise in the process of interpretation, whether the document is medieval literature or the Constitution: high school students are directed toward a preconceived interpretation when teachers ask them to investigate Hemingway's lust for life in *The Old Man and the Sea*. Bork (and the legal community's interpretation of Bork's belief in the Constitution's drafters' "intent") exposed again the nagging problem of establishing meaning. Many of us assume we *know* what something means, and we retreat to the obvious answer of intent to provide ammunition to retain our interpretation.

- A judge guesses at the "intent" of the testator of a disputed will.
- An attorney reads a statute and is convinced of the legislative "intent" behind the statute.
- A client reads your letter and believes you intend to actively pursue his case.

No one can be sure whether these readers are accurate in their interpretations. It is thus the writer's dilemma not only that her audience might misunderstand what she is saying, but also that she herself may have misunderstood the written word (case, statute, memorandum) that stimulated her written response.

Let's focus on the strict denotative function of everyday words. I have gathered a list of those frequently misused; this list cannot overcome the difficulties outlined above, but a writer's recognition of these words may help readers gain access to any text.

---

[2] Zechariah Chafee, Jr., *The Disorderly Conduct of Words*, 41 COLUM. L. REV. 384 (1941).

adapt/adopt: You *adapt* to a situation, accommodating or adjusting to it. You might, on the other hand, *adopt* a position, an amendment, or even a child, meaning you embrace or espouse it.

affect/effect: *Affect* is a verb, meaning to influence or to assume the appearance of. *Effect* is a noun, meaning the *result*.[3]

allusion/illusion: When you refer indirectly to something, you *allude*. *Allusions* in your writing are references to material, ideas, histories that your reader should recognize. *Illusion* is an unreal thing or a false impression.

alternative: If you have two choices, each is an *alternative* to the other. Traditionally, linguists have held that with more than two options, you have *options* or *choices* but not an alternative. Contemporary linguists no longer hold tightly to this distinction.

although/while: Today's dictionaries use these terms synonymously, but the traditional delineation is useful: *while* connotes time and is a temporal signal. *Although* can mean *though* and *even* and *even though*. If the sentence could be mistakenly interpreted to convey the temporal meaning of *while*, careful writers will want to use *although* to avoid possible ambiguity.

among/between: *Among* refers to groups of three and more; *between* functions as a distinction between only two things. (*Among* the many functions of the teaching assistants is the chore of arranging all social functions. *Between* class assignments and work with the freshmen, the teaching assistants have little extra time.)

Between and *among* require objective pronouns: Between you and *me*, I can't stand to witness fights between *him* and *her*. Among *us*, the custom is to bring cookies to the study group once a week.

and/or: Watch out for this form, or you will create ambiguity and confusion. *And* signals *in addition* as a conjunction, a connector of added material. *And* moves items together. *Or* is disjunctive; it presents the alternative or the exclusion.

Both *and* and *or* can be ambiguous, however. *Or* may be inclusive (apples or oranges or both) and exclusive (apples or oranges but not both). "A fine and/or imprisonment" means "a fine or imprisonment or both." To be careful, you can spell out the intended relationship: "or both the fine and imprisonment."

anxious/eager: If you are worried about something, you are *anxious*. If you really want something, you are *eager* for it.

---

[3] *Effect* can be used as a verb, meaning "to make a change" or "to accomplish": He can effect that difference if he talks to both counsel before the trial begins.

as/because: *As* is a comparative, like *like*. *Because* signals causality.

> Incorrect: As he was slow to file all court
> documents, the committee disqualified him.
> Correct: Because he was slow . . .
> The plaintiff can be as sincere as a nun, but
> because she has her dates wrong, she will not be
> believed.

assume/presume: To *assume* is to take for granted that something is true or accurate. To *presume* is to take upon oneself without leave or warrant, to dare or go beyond what is right or proper. Perhaps you can remember the difference by noting the use of the root in *presumption*.

assure/insure/ensure: Because all three words mean to make certain or safe, they cause writing problems. The difference is this: you *assure* people. *Assure* implies removing all doubt and suspense from someone's mind. You *insure* with money, guarantees, and (insurance) policies. And you *ensure* when you are making a thing certain and inevitable, making the outcome sure.

bequeath/devise: In traditional legal writing, you can *bequeath* personal property, like cars and jewelry, but you *devise* real (estate) property.

bimonthly/semimonthly: Enough confusion exists about these words that most writers resort to using "every two months" or "twice a month." *Bi* means two; *semi* means half. Thus, *bimonthly* is every two months and *semimonthly* is twice a month.

case: *Case* has a definite use in legal language; therefore, it is best to reserve it for the precedent, the earlier situation before the court. Rather than using the word casually ("in any case," "it is frequently the case that"), replace it with more concrete alternatives (*often, frequently, from any perspective*). Remember also that the case is not the court. You simply cannot say "The case decided . . . ." The court or the judge may have decided.

cite: *Cite* as a verb is used in legal jargon as a verb to refer to legal authority, meaning "to mention in support of." The noun form, *citation*, has somehow been transformed into a verb that is familiar to all legal scholars but few laypersons.

clearly: *Clearly* is an overused and misused throat clearer. If something is already *clear*, marking it as such is merely redundant. If the idea is not clear, marking it *clear* will only draw attention to it. A number of judges ask their clerks to read through the briefs looking for any argument tagged with *clearly*; they assume that argument is weak and needed linguistic support.

continual/continuous: *Continual* means frequently occurring; *continuous* means occurring without interference. The professor gave a two-hour, *continuous* lecture. A disgruntled student on the back row offered *continual* interruptions.

credible/credulous: If the evidence is *credible*, it is believable. But the victim of the swindle was *credulous*, because she "believed too readily" and thus was gullible. Similarly, in the negative, an *incredible* testimony is not believable, and an *incredulous* jury was disbelieving and skeptical.

currently/presently: Although *current* and *present*, as nouns, are basically synonymous, the adverb forms traditionally signal a difference in time. We are *currently* (right now) studying word choice. *Presently* (in the very near future) we will stop and take a break.

different from/different than: Things *differ from* each other. *Different than* is considered "incorrect" unless the preferred form creates bulky, illogical phraseology following it.

```
Black's argument is different from White's.
I agree that the Supreme Court has interpreted the
United States Constitution very differently than
the Founders intended and that courts err on the
side of tyranny. [A rewrite to replace "differ-
ently than" would be wordier: "I agree that the
Supreme Court has interpreted the United States
Constitution differently from the way that the
Founders intended and that courts err on the side
of tyranny."]
```

discreet/discrete: A *discreet* investigator is tactful and judicious, careful. An investigator may be *discrete* from other witnesses at the trial, meaning that he is disconnected from them, separate and distinct.

disinterested/uninterested: These words are surprisingly different. A judge or stenographer is *disinterested* in a case; that is, the judge has no personal involvement in it and yet needs to know the details of the case. The court clerk may truly be *uninterested*, that is, not engaged by the elements of the story: Because the clerk was totally *uninterested* in the proceeding, the fact that she fell asleep was not surprising.

elicit/illicit: To *elicit* help in the fund drive, an attorney is calling forth, bringing out, evoking. The *illicit* use of funds, though, is a use that is not permitted or is unlawful.

explicit/implicit: The literal sense of these words makes them opposites; colloquial misuse has created confusion, so the careful writer might need to use synonyms for the two words: *explicit* means expressed, and *implicit* means implied.

famous/notorious: Litigator Gary Spence is *famous* for his voir dire, meaning he is well known for a positive trait; Charles Manson is *notorious* for mass murders in California, which indicates fame, yes, but for a pejorative and unpleasant reason.

farther/further: Careful writers save *farther* for actual distance and *further* to mean "to a greater extent."

finding: *Finding* is the determination of an issue of fact. Do not slip into using *finding* as a replacement for *holding*, which refers to matters of law.

herein: *Herein* is supposed to direct the attention of the reader to the material within the document; confusion has resulted in its use, however, because it has been interpreted variously to mean "anywhere within this document" and also more narrowly, including "here within this section (or paragraph)." If you use the word, be specific about its antecedent.

historic/historical: A *historic* occasion is momentous, one that will make history. If the event already belongs in the past, it is *historical*, as are historical novels that thus deal with past events. A side issue here is "*a* historic" versus "*an* historic." In America, we sound out our *h*'s. So unless you are willing to consistently write "an hot date" or "an hysterical moment," you need to use the *a* before *historic*.

hopefully: *Hopefully* is an adverb meaning "with hope." Tradition required a writer to narrow the definition to that adverbial definition: "Hopefully, it will rain" would thus be ambiguous suggesting either that it is going to rain hope or that the speaker is hoping it rains. Today's usage dictionaries now allow for this ambiguity, adding to the traditional definition of *hopefully* "I or we hope." If you retain the traditional definition, you can avoid the ambiguity.

i.e./e.g.: *I.e.,* an abbreviation of *id est*, means "that is" and indicates that an inclusive list or statement will follow. *E.g.* (*exempli gratia*), means "for example" and signals that the author is including an example or examples with the introductory statement.

```
I like literature; i.e., I read everything I can
get my hands on.
```

```
I like literature; e.g., I am reading all of
John Barth this month and plan to begin adventure
books that reflect the Zen attitude next month.
```

imply/implicate: *To imply* is to hint at something. *To implicate* is to suggest an intimate or incriminating connection.

```
He implied that she was not telling the truth
when he asked to see her list of references.
     He implicated her in the jewelry case by admit-
ting he knew her car and schedule.
```

imply/infer: *To imply* is to hint at something, usually to insinuate. *To infer* is to deduce, to figure something out.

in behalf of/on behalf of: To give a charitable party *in behalf of* a children's organization is to give the party to benefit it. To give a speech *on behalf of* your law firm would be to speak as a representative of the firm.

involve: Language purists save *involve* to mean "to implicate or to entangle."

```
Correct: The incident involved several major law
firms.
     Incorrect: This is a case involving a trust fund
and the purchase of a new home. [The case is not
necessarily entangling the fund. Instead, "In this
case a loan officer misapplied a trust fund toward
the purchase of a new home."]
```

it: *It* is a pronoun for an ungendered or non-sexed antecedent. When you are referring to a defendant, *he* or *she* or *they* is appropriate unless your defendant happens to be a company or institution. Briefs and memoranda are dehumanized enough without the following kind of sentence:

```
Incorrect: The defendant was aerially spraying an
easement which it owned when the spray drifted
onto plaintiff's land. [If Mr. Jones owns the
plane, use he. If International Aircraft owns the
plane, it is appropriate.]
```

its/it's: *It's* easy to distinguish these two forms if you can remember that the apostrophe signals that a letter is left out, so the form *it's* must stand for "it is." Following that rule will force its competitor, *its*, into its only logical slot, as a third-person singular pronoun.

like/as: *Like* and *as* are not interchangeable. Use *like* to precede a noun *not* followed by a verb. Use *as* to precede a noun plus verb:

```
Winston tastes good as a cigarette should.
He can throw a ball like a professional.
```

literally: *Literally* means exactly what it says. You might inadvertently use it instead of *figuratively,* which actually means "not literally."

me, you, him, her, it/myself, yourself, himself, herself, itself: Writers unsure of pronoun case (nominative, objective, reflexive) occasionally mischoose the reflexive for the objective.

```
Incorrect: They gave the award to Joe and myself.
Correct: They gave the award to Joe and me.
```

moot: *Moot* has two opposite meanings! Academically, it means "arguable," hence the moot courts where students argue fictitious cases. But it also means "no longer subject to argument." So you will read and write about courts that dismiss cases "by reason of mootness."

only: *Only* emphasizes or modifies the word immediately following it. You can trace its effect on a sentence by examining the example below:

```
The attorney sent him the will yesterday.
```

Now watch what happens if I move that four-letter word into the sentence:

```
    Only the attorney [no one else, not the execu-
tor, parents, etc.] sent him the will yesterday.
    The only attorney [no other attorney was in-
volved] sent him the will yesterday.
    The attorney only sent [implies that she didn't
call or talk with him] him the will yesterday.
    The attorney sent only him [not anyone else] the
will yesterday.
    The attorney sent him only the will [didn't send
anything else] yesterday.
```

```
The attorney sent him the will only yesterday
[implies recently, moment near at hand as opposed
to long ago].
     The attorney sent him the will yesterday only
[illogically implies that there were multiple, op-
tional days for the sending and she didn't send it
out on consecutive days].
```

Other words have the same effect when they are mislocated: *even, hardly, scarcely, merely, nearly, never, not, almost, just, quite.*

oral/verbal: "Of the mouth" is *oral*: I can have *oral* surgery on Friday. "In, by, or of words" is *verbal*. I can *verbally* reprimand my children or raise my eyebrow and silently reprimand them.

oversight: *Oversight* can mean both "unintentional error" and "intentional watchful supervision."

```
     The motion was filed later because of a clerical
oversight.
     The oversight of the ethics committee will
change the practice of many members of the bar.
```

perpetual/prolonged: Rip Van Winkle awoke from a *prolonged* sleep to discover that the colonies were now an independent country. If he had fallen into a *perpetual* sleep, which means unceasing, he would never have awoken.

possible/practicable: *Possible* is within the limits of ability, capacity, something that may or may not occur. *Practicable*, on the other hand, applies to things feasible, usable, but that have not been tested.

prescribe/proscribe: You *prescribe* when you are giving a remedy or a decree. The opposite is true of *proscribe*, when you are forbidding, prohibiting.

reluctant/reticent: If your witness is *reluctant* to testify, she is unwilling or will grudgingly consent. That she is *reticent*, however, means she does not reveal her feelings readily.

rule: *Rule* differs from *holding* in that a judge *rules* on motions and objections to evidence. On the other hand, though, he *holds* in favor of the plaintiff or defendant.

since/because: Traditionally these words were different enough that they were not interchangeable, as they are becoming today. Although it is not incorrect to use them interchangeably, it is to a lawyer's benefit to maintain the traditional distinction because they create different expectations. *Since* can mean both *because* and the passage of time; it is both temporal and causal. *Because*, however, signals only causality. Thus, legal writers who reserve *since* to signal time eliminate the need for rereading:

```
    Ambiguous: Since this provision has been reen-
acted, the agency has received the criminal his-
tory of the application. [Because it has been
reenacted? or since that time?]
    Clear: Because he ran over the plaintiff, she
has been unable to walk for three months.
```

state: *State* is not an automatic synonym for *say*, but means "to express concisely and fully." Judges do not all have to *state*. Some say, observe, notice, opine.

```
    Your terms will be stated in writing.
    Please state your demands.
```

that/which: If you draft an essential (restrictive) clause that will not be punctuated "out" of the sentence with commas, use *that*. If the clause is meant to be nonessential, relatively unnecessary to the sentence's meaning, use two commas and *which*.

```
    The clause that you need the most is not
punctuated.
    The clause, which is not essential to the sen-
tence, disappeared from the eye when it was set
off with commas.
```

this/that: *This* and *that* are ambiguous pronouns when left to themselves, away from their antecedents. Follow them with concrete nouns: *That* issue is too complex for *this* type of response.

where: *Where* can mean "when," "if," "because," "in which," and "that." Legal writers overuse poor *where* so often that readers frequently do not know what the writer is saying.

```
    Unclear: where one party is guilty . . . [Readers
are left wondering if the writer means if one
party is guilty, or maybe the place one party is
guilty, or maybe even when one party is guilty.]
```

If legal writers reserve *where* to signal location, readers will be able to follow more easily, especially in the "Questions Presented" sections of memoranda that sometimes begin, according to convention, with *where*.

who/which: If your antecedent is inanimate (nonhuman), use *that* or *which* as a pronoun. If the antecedent is a person, use *who*. The question becomes more complicated when you are referring to your client, for instance, an agency filled with people. If you are referring to the agency (client group) as a whole, use *which*; if the people within the agency are the center of your sentence or its intent, use *who* and *whom*.

> Correct: The factfinders of the agency, who are
> veteran questioners, believe the client has previ-
> ous fraudulent claims.
>
> Correct: The initiating agency, which inquired
> about the status of our jurisdiction, has been
> satisfied through an earlier memorandum.
>
> Incorrect: Grades are a tag and weight fastened
> on you by the faculty, which determine exactly how
> high in the legal world you are going to rise at
> graduation. [Like any relative or demonstrative
> pronoun, which should refer to the closest logical
> antecedent. Perhaps here the antecedent is "fac-
> ulty"; more likely, it is "tag and weight."]

V

PUNCTUATING
FOR CLARITY
The Poetry of Punctuation

22

ALLOWING COMMAS TO CREATE MEANING

Punctuation should signal the intended meaning, emphasis, and relationships among the words of the sentences and paragraph. If writers do not use punctuation marks to support their meaning, they create tension like a car does when it soars down a street with no brakes at all not a foot brake or handbrake and the passersby have to worry about their safety.

Unnecessary punctuation marks, on the other hand, disrupt meaning and produce choppy prose, like someone trying out car brakes after a storm and tapping, stomping, tapping, again, on the way to the corner. He, eventually, gets where he is going, but his passenger is shaken, exhausted, by the experience, just like the reader of this sentence.

Useful punctuation causes a quick pause or a complete stop at appropriate moments. Our first records of Western punctuation indicate that punctuation began about A.D. 3 to signal pauses for orators: to help readers pause, marks above, in the middle, and below the line of letters signaled different pause lengths. Later, Benedictine monks recorded early Western culture with an erratic system of punctuation. As literacy developed, clergy and, later, clerks used words and punctuation to suit developing needs. Interestingly, punctuation as a set of rules did not exist until the 1700s, when many aspects of society became codified.

Since then, punctuation has reflected its contemporary society: during the Victorian age, society was strict about all conventions, including punctuation, for which the Victorians codified "rules." Today's society, on the other hand, has little codified structure or defined mores. Thus, writing advice varies: "If you 'hear' a pause, add a comma." Other teachers, reflecting different societal priorities, intone, "When in doubt, leave it [comma] out." Even punctuation experts are not convinced or convincing; the last widely acknowledged expert, George Summey, published *American Punctuation* in 1919, and he was more laissez-faire than prescriptive. His suggestions were based on the investigation of popular newsprint for community habits rather than an insistence on adherence to any particular school of thought.

The most ambiguous punctuation mark is the comma, that slip of a mark. Unlike the period, with its authoritative, commanding "halt!" or the semicolon, with its invitation to join two similar ideas within two independent clauses, the comma is a subtlety, a suggestion of a stop, a pause, a slight consideration. It is thus more sophisticated than a period and more difficult to master because it expresses not the gross messages we wish to convey but the gentle, subtle turns of our minds, of our expressions. Pico Iyer, *Times* essayist, describes the role of the "humble comma" this way:

> A world that has only periods is a world without inflections. It is a world without shade. It has a music without sharps and flats. It is a martial music. It has a jackboot rhythm. Words cannot bend and curve. A comma, by comparison, catches the gentle drift of the mind in thought, turning in on itself and back on itself, reversing, redoubling and returning along the course of its own sweet river music; while the semicolon brings clauses and thoughts together with all the silent discretion of a hostess arranging guests around her dinner table.[1]

Whatever your response to this concept of comma as nobility, you have to admit that commas carry a certain power—they pull readers through difficult material, they delineate between pieces of ideas, they stop the eye at appropriate moments. The question has to be, "What is an appropriate moment?" Notice the license Iyer takes with the semicolon after "music": a simple comma would have been technically correct, but he chose a semicolon for further delineation.

---

[1] Pico Iyer, *That Humble Comma*, TIME, June 13, 1988, at 80.

NO ABSOLUTE RULES

Few punctuation rules are absolute. Contemporary creative writers break every conventional punctuation rule for stylistic purposes. Thus, today's standard "rules" are more likely to be stylistic suggestions than requirements, except in the law. In the segment of society controlled by stare decisis and detail-oriented judges, legal writers necessarily lean toward a narrower, more traditional sense of punctuation because the consequences of a loose or sloppy construction are so grim. Legal writers face an interesting dilemma: on the one hand, they need to follow traditional rules that governed earlier legal writers—for the sake of continuity and for the sake of judges who must compare earlier statutes and rules to contemporary, changing rules and legal quandaries. But, on the other hand, legal writers want to produce a prose that the consumer-audience can understand.

This tension creates a schizophrenia: fighting archaic jargon and formatted incantations, legal writers simply do not have the energy or interest to fight the changing rules for punctuation.

Unfortunately, though, punctuation is an integral part of prose, and legal writers are nagged by fears of committing a stylistic error that can change substantive text. Good paragraphs and good sentences are grouped and coordinated, subordinated, listed, held together, and broken apart by punctuation. Legal ideas are reflected in the punctuation drafters choose. Rather than give up on following today's shifting rules for punctuation, legal writers need a simple standard for punctuation marks. The rules and examples below may help narrow the confusion about the comma, undoubtedly the most difficult mark to master.

CONSTRUCTION WITH SPECIFIC RULES

Do not place a single comma between the subject and its verb.

Incorrect: The oath, however must be administered in a manner acceptable to the U.S. courts. [One comma separates the subject of the sentence, "oath," from its verb, "must be administered." Interrupters like "however" require a comma on both sides, much as parentheses signal the beginning and conclusion of other parentheticals.]

Do not place a single comma between the verb and its object.

> Incorrect: The federal courts have stated, that
> the attorney-client privilege consists of five
> specific elements. [A comma after the verb
> "stated" separates it from the object-clause be-
> ginning with "that" and thus miscues readers who
> may think that the courts have first stated, and
> then done something else, too, perhaps "ruled."]

**Do not place a single comma between the verb and its adver-
bial clause.**

> Incorrect: In these cases, the Texas Supreme
> Court has been strict in limiting the trial
> court's discretion, because "[t]he rules of dis-
> covery were changed to prevent trials by ambush
> and to ensure that fairness would prevail."

Occasionally writers will deliberately choose to break this rule to emphasize and set apart the adverbial clause:

> Mr. Brown is indeed a victim of police brutal-
> ity, if brutality includes a shove to force some-
> one into a police car.

**Use a comma after an introductory adverbial clause; adverbial
clauses placed at the end of the sentence or next to the verb do not
take a comma:**

> If Mr. Brown can prove that he was falsely ar-
> rested and that he was struck without provocation,
> he will be entitled to relief under the 14th
> Amendment of the Constitution.
> Mr. Brown will be entitled to relief under the
> 14th Amendment of the Constitution if he can prove
> that he was falsely arrested and that he was
> struck without provocation.

**Do not place a comma in a date that states only the month and year;
use a comma before and after the year if the date includes the day:**

In July 1989 the banks insisted on liquidation
of the Millers' assets; by December 15, 1989, the
Millers' assets were liquid.

**For quotations, place a comma after an introductory word when it
introduces an independent clause; omit the comma after an introductory word when the quotation becomes an integral part of the
textual sentence's syntax.**

Incorrect: The letter has an instruction identi-
cal to the one under question except that it includes, "presented at our bank at 5000 Lamar."

Correct: The court replied, "The plaintiff must
show a reasonable probability that the parties
would enter into a contractual relationship."

Correct: The courts have held that "[t]he
plaintiff must show a reasonable probability
that the parties would enter into a contractual
relationship."

Place commas inside quotation marks:

The plaintiff must show that the defendant
"acted maliciously," that the defendant was not
privileged, and that "actual harm or damage oc-
curred as a result of the interference."

ADDITIONAL RULES FOR LEGAL WRITERS

**Place a comma between two independent clauses separated by a
conjunction.**

Incorrect: The out-of-control car hit the child
and the dog ran over to investigate. [This sort of
confusion in a piece of fiction would merely force
the reader to reread; in legal writing, with its
embedded clauses and multiple subjects, the missing comma creates substantive ambiguity. A comma
between the two independent clauses signals closure of one idea; the immediately following and or
or signals the close relationship between the two

clauses. This rule is broken more often for independent clauses connected by <u>and</u> than by <u>or</u>, perhaps because <u>or</u> is disjunctive and needs further
separation.]

Place commas between all items in a series.

<u>Incorrect:</u> He was charged with assault and bat-
tery, breaking and entering and rape. [Omitting
the final comma in the series confuses the disparate entities: in legal writing, it is more important to be clear than to save the space of a
comma.]

<u>Correct:</u> The girl wanted to see all the evidence,
hear the testimony, and read the depositions.

CONSTRUCTION OPEN TO OPTIONS

Use or omit the comma after a beginning phrase:

In July of 1955 the bank signed three security
agreements for this business.
In July of 1955, the bank signed three security
agreements for this business.

The trend today is toward less punctuation. Probably introductory
phrases should be punctuated only when a lack of punctuation creates
ambiguity.

Use commas to set off descriptive phrases and absolutes depending on the author's meaning:

My aunt the swimmer was injured last week. [The
author has more than one aunt, so the "swimmer"
absolute cannot have commas separating it. Instead, the description is essential to distinguish
"which one" about the noun.]

My aunt, the swimmer, was injured last week. [Of
importance to the author was the aunt's injury.
That she is a swimmer was not essential and therefore could be set off with a comma on each side.]

23
SENTENCE PUNCTUATION GUIDE

Legal writers who know they have problems with punctuation can use the following summary as a visual/graphic guide. Quick-help guides like this one have long aided conscientious writing students with the memorization and application of those pesky punctuation marks that create rhetorical chaos if they are misapplied.

1. Complete sentence.
2. Complete sentence   , and   complete sentence.
                                           , or
                                           , nor
                                           , but
                                           , yet
                                           , for
3. Complete sentence; complete sentence.
4. Complete sentence;   therefore,   complete sentence.
                                       however,
                                       nevertheless,
                                       consequently,
                                       furthermore,
                                       moreover,
5. Complete   , on the other hand,   sentence.
                                   , for example,
                                   , in fact,

6. Although   incomplete sentence,   complete sentence.
   After
   Because
   Since
   Before
   When
   While

7. Complete sentence   although   incomplete sentence.
   after
   because
   since
   before
   during
   when
   while

8. Complete sentence: 1, 2, and 3.

9. "Yes," the plaintiff said. [quotation—comma—complete sentence]

10. The defendant countered, "No." [complete sentence—comma—quotation]

11. The defendant countered, "No"; complete sentence. [complete sentence—comma—quotation—semicolon—complete sentence]

12. The defendant countered, "No": 1, 2, and 3. [complete sentence—comma—quotation—colon—list—period]

The following sentences exemplify the above patterns:

```
1. The defendant looked toward the plaintiff.
2. The defendant looked toward the plaintiff, and
   then he pointed at her.
3. The defendant looked toward the plaintiff; he
   pointed at her.
4. The defendant looked toward the plaintiff;
   furthermore, he pointed at her.
5. The defendant looked, of course, toward the
   plaintiff.
6. After looking toward the plaintiff, the defendant
   then pointed at her.
7. The defendant pointed at the plaintiff after look-
   ing at her for a while.
```

8. The defendant listed three retaliatory grievances:
   she lied about her marital status, she neglected
   to mention she had no license or insurance, and
   she omitted her police record.
9. "It's not my fault that she did all that first,"
   the defendant countered.
10. The defendant countered, "It's not my fault that
    she did all that first."
11. The defendant countered, "It's not my fault that
    she did all that first"; the plaintiff naturally
    disagreed.
12. The defendant countered the plaintiff's attack
    with a list of three "sins of omission": not list-
    ing her marital status, not explaining her lack of
    license or insurance, and not reporting her police
    record on the application form.

When future archaeologists unearth American texts, they won't require a Rosetta Stone to decipher our grammar—it's fairly easy. But surely they'll be stumped by all the odd permutations of punctuation around our " " " " 's!

24
"QUOTATION MARKS?"
She Queried—or,
The Arbitrary Rules
Surrounding
Quotation Marks

Which of these sentences is correctly punctuated?

1. The history of the mineral rights to the Canadian well is listed in "Exhibit A".
2. Wall Street's Sullivan & Cromwell could become the first law firm to be acquired by a "financial services conglomerate:" Shearson Lehman/American Express.
3. The drafters who wrote Rule 1.3 of the ABA's Model Rules of Professional Conduct suggested "reasonable diligence", but they did not provide a definition or guidelines for "reasonable".
4. The judge looked at the fifteen-page motion and asked, "What could possibly be new in this case"?
5. Society has an interest in ensuring that genetic testing is "properly performed and interpreted;" negligence in the performance of genetic testing would fail both the individuals involved and society at large.

6. How can the law be efficient and certain without resorting to sweeping generalizations such as "Death to all thieves?"

If you answered "none," you have learned the arbitrary uses of conventional punctuation marks around quotation marks. The conventions for quotation marks do not follow a system of logic. Most other grammar and punctuation rules begin with a need for grammatical precision; someone develops a formula that addresses the need, and that formula attempts to eliminate the initial obscurity. Unfortunately, this logical process was skipped when punctuation rules for quotation marks developed.

Summary of the American rules governing the punctuation surrounding quotation marks:

> **Commas and periods belong inside the quotation marks.**
> **Colons and semicolons belong outside the quotation marks.**
>
> **Question marks and exclamation points are placed according to the meaning of the sentence.**

Corrected versions of the above examples would look like this:

1. The history of the mineral rights to the Canadian well is listed in "Exhibit A."
2. Wall Street's Sullivan & Cromwell could become the first law firm to be acquired by a "financial services conglomerate": Shearson Lehman/American Express.
3. The drafters who wrote Rule 1.3 of the ABA's Model Rules of Professional Conduct suggested "reasonable diligence," but they did not provide a definition or guidelines for "reasonable."
4. The judge looked at the fifteen-page motion and asked, "What could possibly be new in this case?"
5. Society has an interest in ensuring that genetic testing is "properly performed and interpreted"; negligence in the performance of genetic testing would fail both the individuals involved and society at large.
6. How can the law be efficient and certain without resorting to sweeping generalizations such as "Death to all thieves"?

Given the irregular and illogical nature of these rules, writers might be tempted to write without using quotation marks at all—handling this punctuation the way some writers handle the comma. Unfortunately, quotation marks are necessary even for "minimalist" writers, although the *Bluebook*[1] has reduced legal writers' problems by eliminating most of the traditional uses of quotation marks. Standard, nonlegal writers use quotation marks for article titles; they also have the option of using them to emphasize a word or phrase and to identify a word or phrase that is itself the subject of discussion.

The *Bluebook*, interested in the typography of the legal page, has replaced several traditional uses of quotation marks with italics or underlining. For emphasis, or for identifying a word treated as a word, the *Bluebook* underlines or italicizes.

Traditional: The words "imply" and "infer" are not synonymous any more than "ego" and "super-ego" are.

Bluebook: The words imply and infer are not synonymous any more than ego and superego are.

For titles of short, collected works, the *Bluebook* underlines or italicizes.

Traditional: In her 1951 collection, A Change of World, Adrienne Rich attempted to etch the boundaries of art within the larger mosaic of emotional life. In "At a Bach Concert" she wrote: "A too-compassionate art is half an art. / Only such proud restraining purity / Restores the else-betrayed, too-human heart." [Short poems and collected works are punctuated with quotation marks; book titles and works published independently are underlined.]

Bluebook: This exposure was deliberate and well-timed. Russell Baker, The Beer Culture, N.Y. Times, May 27, 1980, at A27, col. 2. [An article in a periodical is underlined or italicized, as is a book title. Names of periodicals are neither underlined nor put into quotation marks. The rules

---

[1] A UNIFORM SYSTEM OF CITATION (15th ed. 1991).

are different yet again if the material appears in
a law review, which has a unique typeface, large
and small capital letters, for various components
in the footnotes.]

The differences between traditional style and legal style underscore the arbitrary nature of punctuation. As long as the audience agrees
on the same signals for specific pauses and titles, then the physical nature of the actual punctuation mark is incidental. The problem, of
course, is that audience awareness must occur before audience agreement. In this case, legal writers first have to understand what the *Bluebook* advocates and how it differs from traditional typography. Only
then can they consistently follow another arbitrary system.

Legal writers use quotation marks in limited, but specific situations: for definitions and for direct quotations.

DEFINITIONS

In this brief, "RoCo" refers to the Rotary Rota-
tion Company.

In this contract, "Buyer" will refer only to the
participants listed in the first paragraph.

"Exhibit A" provides the court with an overview
of the budget.

From the <u>Bluebook:</u> <u>Contra</u>: Cited authority <u>di-
rectly states the contrary</u> of the position. "<u>Con-
tra</u>" is used where "[no signal]" would be used for
support.[2] [Note that the <u>Bluebook</u> resorts to both
italics and quotation marks in this example: <u>Con-
tra</u> requires italics because it is used as a signal, and it is also a word the editors want to
emphasize.][3]

DIRECT QUOTATIONS

Attorneys make frequent use of quotations in both memoranda and
briefs and thus confront the problem of punctuating around both textual and block quotations.

---

[2] *Id.* rule 1.2(c), at 23.
[3] See *id.* rule 1, at 21–23, rule 7(a), at 49.

> Textual quotation: U.S. District Judge Jack B.
> Weinstein described the language of Medicare
> benefit form letters: "The language used is bu-
> reaucratic gobbledygook, jargon, double-talk, a
> form of officialese, federalese, and insurancese
> and doublespeak. It does not qualify as English."

If attorneys follow the *Bluebook* advice, they indent quotations longer than fifty words and do not enclose the words in quotation marks.

> Block quotation: Thus, this case revolves around
> the funding sources of the two candidates. The
> Election Campaign Finance Act provides specific
> limitations for contributions:
>
>   Sec. 31 (a) Except as provided in subsection
> (b), a person other than a campaign committee
> shall not make contributions on behalf of the
> winner of a primary election for the office of
> governor in excess of $600 for any purpose after
> the date of such primary election.
>
>   (b) A contribution from a member of a candi-
> date's immediate family to the campaign commit-
> tee for that candidate is exempt from the limi-
> tation of subsection (a).
>
>   (c) As used in subsection (b), "immediate
> family" means a spouse, parent, brother, sister,
> son, or daughter.

Quotation of a complete sentence is preceded by a comma or
a colon, depending on whether the quotation is introduced formally.
Either way, though, the first word is capitalized because both the textual
sentence and the quotation are complete sentences:

>   The court concluded, "The number of judges can-
> not keep up with the demands of society."
>
>   The court summarized the problem as follows: "In
> less than two decades, the total number of filings
> in California has increased 176 percent in the
> Supreme Court and 438 percent in the Court of
> Appeals."

If the quotation is less than a complete sentence, it is not preceded by punctuation and the first word is not capitalized:

> Scott Turow, in <u>One L.</u> says that if a female attorney appears before the court, the competitive nature of the law causes trouble because "a gentleman is not supposed to feel at ease in combat with a lady."
>
> The court concluded that "[t]he number of judges cannot keep up with the demands of society."

UNAUTHORIZED DEVIATION

In spite of these generally accepted conventions for legal punctuation, a curious practice has developed throughout the legal profession that has no parallel in other written work: some attorneys both indent long, direct quotations and use quotation marks around them. Some legal writers admit that they deliberately deviate from the *Bluebook* to emphasize the quotation. These writers are inadvertently admitting that their writing is frequently nothing more than long lists of excerpted opinions strung together. To differentiate between the bulky quotations and the meager text, legal writers use the double signal to highlight information from the outside sources. The result is that unique legal look: long sheets of double- (or even single-) spaced print, with the majority of the lines indented. Quotation marks are scattered liberally—and incorrectly.

The double signal is a crutch; rather than developing prose that incorporates quotations into their own textual argument, the writers stack quotations together and add neon signs, superfluous quotation marks. They rely on the quotations to make their argument and therefore rely on the double signal to flash the information to the reader. If writers instead incorporate the legal precedent into their textual argument, they do not have to depend on punctuation to make their prose point. Punctuation is then relegated to its only logical role, that of a supportive, mechanical aid.

25

THAT SOPHISTICATED SEMICOLON

Never using a semicolon is like refusing to use a computer; the technology is there waiting to make life easier, but fear keeps the writers from turning on the computer. Never using a semicolon is similar to writing without using your full vocabulary; if you develop a full arsenal of word options, they can add subtle layers of meaning. Never using a semicolon condemns punctuation to a sameness as dull as using the same sentence structure repeatedly. If you have avoided them in the past, then take the plunge and learn the very few rules for semicolons.

The rules for semicolons are simple and unambiguous:

Use a semicolon to replace a period between two complete sentences.

The period within the punctuation mark signals the end of a complete sentence; the comma below the period is the writer's signal for a strong connection between the two ideas of the two sentences:

> He writes the worst English that I have ever
> encountered. It reminds me of a string of wet
> sponges; it reminds me of tattered washing on the
> line; it reminds me of stale bean soup, of college
> yells, of dogs barking idiotically through endless

```
nights. It is so bad that a sort of grandeur
creeps into it.¹
```

Use a semicolon to delineate items in a series that are already marked by other descriptive commas.

Semicolons in these limited instances function like *big* commas to distinguish groups of words that already contain commas. Thus, like an architect who can offer a floor plan, full of options; who can tailor interior details to various tastes, like your age and your community and your social status; and who can provide landscape with minimal care and Chinese simplicity or Elizabethan splendor, a writer can use the semicolon to separate elements of a sentence with skill. Like the architect, the writer delineates like elements into like units:

```
Allowed into the deposition will be a stenog-
rapher, Cathy Haggard; attorney John Smith;
the plaintiff, Ed Jones; and the plaintiff's
attorneys.
```

```
Without the necessary semicolons: Allowed into the
deposition will be a stenographer, Cathy Haggard,
attorney John Smith, the plaintiff, Ed Jones, and
the plaintiff's attorneys.
```

Without the semicolons, readers cannot tell that the stenographer in the above example is Cathy Haggard or that the plaintiff is Ed Jones, because the commas that help to make subordinate descriptions (appositives) are too easily confused with commas that function to co-ordinate the major elements—that is, which people are allowed in the deposition. On first reading of the example with only commas, the commas appear to coordinate equal items. But they do not. Some signal subordinate modification (the stenographer, Cathy Haggard), while other commas try to coordinate parallel items in a series (the list of who is allowed). The poor little comma simply is not up to both tasks at once. That is when semicolons take over.

---

¹H. L. Mencken, *Gamalielese*, Baltimore Evening Sun, Mar. 7, 1921, quoted in Impossible H. L. Mencken: A Selection of his Best Newspaper Stories 407–408 (Marion E. Rodgers ed., 1991).

Some writers worry that semicolons project a high degree of formality and that using them would impart an air of formality, of haughtiness, to a document, which may be true, if readers notice them at all. If you examine *USA Today* and cartoons, you will indeed find fewer semicolons than you will in an essay from *Harper's* or *The New York Times Book Review*. The increased number of semicolons is an interesting reflection of the complexity of thought. The more important it is to express connections between ideas, the more important the semicolon becomes. Perhaps, therefore, legal writers might avoid semicolons in a dunning letter, but they would use them in a brief to make persuasive connections between precedent and a current case.

Semicolons offer a delightful push and pull; a yin and yang; an offer to come hither, but not yet. They promise just a little bit more about the ideas before them. It is as if the period within the semicolon first requires that readers stop and digest, but then it entices them onward: the period component of a semicolon is like a hostess who sits contentedly, encouraging her guests to eat the last morsel of the third course; through smile and gesture and even the placement of her silverware, she manages to offer a promise of the next course to come. That's a part of the semicolon. The balancing part of the semicolon is the comma beneath the period that encourages connections: it is like an experienced widower on a date who knows he must stop for the moment but nevertheless wants to entice and encourage his date toward the future. The complete mark, the period atop the comma, is the total sum of its two components. That widower is unlike a nervous teenager who would either give up and stop completely (like any period within two sentences) or would rush on with only a little pause (like a comma). Like a sophisticated widower, a sophisticated hostess, the writer can use the semicolon as the mark of simultaneously pausing and continuing.

Writers who begin to enjoy the nuance of semicolons can move beyond the two rules into the optional uses of semicolons that offer a more casual pause-but-go. As early as 1919, American punctuation specialist George Summey categorized the more flamboyant use of semicolons as a deliberate replacement for commas and dashes. Semicolons can be used to suggest that a second group of words is coordinated with the first:

```
He tried to get the court to extend the deadline;
the mailman to make a special trip; his secretary
to make a run to the courthouse.
```

This example is not technically, formally correct, because a comma would suffice and the semicolon here presents readers with sentence ellipses, or fragments. The concluding phrases are not independent sentences (see the first rule above), nor do they contain internal commas that require semicolons to create coordinate and subordinate groups (see the second rule above). But the above example is not incorrect either, because readers can easily enough add the necessary missing elements to the final phrases. In this example, the writer has chosen to force readers to stop a little longer than a simple comma would ask. Thus he has manipulated the punctuation to help his points become more emphatic in a nontraditional manner. It works. Used carefully and deliberately, the semicolon can become a sophisticated signal for pause-but-go.

The careful use of semicolons becomes another opportunity to dictate reader speed; they encourage the eye forward but yet can be a temporary resting spot amid clauses and conditionals, among the textual blast of words and minor chords of the comma; between intricate sentences, the semicolon provides a pause.

Rather than writing without a computer, a full vocabulary, or varied sentence structure, legal writers should take advantage of every tool available, including the semicolon. Build parallel structures like an architect; serve up words like a careful hostess; display wisdom and sophistication like a widower. Use the semicolon.

26
COMPOUND ADJECTIVES AND NOUN STRINGS

Readers process either word by word or, preferably, unit by unit of words. We do not need to be psychologists or reading specialists to understand that the mind recognizes groups—words, prepositional phrases, parallel construction, or any other traditional glue—as it skips to the next word or unit of words. One of the many tensions writers face is the balance between the unconnected words in a sentence (and thus a staccato, hard-to-follow jumble) and elongated strings of overly enmeshed words. Thus, sophisticated writers tinker with their words, creating units where necessary and breaking up overextended ones.

CREATING UNITS

One word unit that can help readers is a compound adjective before a noun. The two adjectives combine and should be processed together. These compound adjective units differ from two separate adjectives describing a noun: *Delighted and curious*, the baby reached for the shining bubble in the water. In this example, the two adjectives obviously both describe, independently, the baby.

Compound adjectives, on the other hand, use one adjective to modify a second adjective: *sixteenth-century novelist*. The novelist is not sixteenth, of course; the century is. The writer uses an intervening hyphen to signal the modifying relationship, helping readers to both assimilate the adjectives properly and anticipate the subsequent noun.

When they create these compound-adjectival units, writers should not neglect the necessary hyphen, because the result can be ambiguity or even error; nevertheless, trying to appear conservative and to keep from littering their pages with hyphens, many writers hesitate to use the hyphen. They write "private coin operated telephones." But do they mean private coins that operate telephones? or worse, "operated telephones of private coins"? Readers have to process the phrase twice to grasp the meaning unless they are already familiar with the entity that the unit represents. A simple hyphen would resolve the confusion: private coin-operated telephones.

A hesitancy to use hyphens is not the only reason so many of these units go unpunctuated. It is difficult for writers to be aware of these compound adjectives because the subject matter is familiar as a unit. Writers *see* the words as the unit they represent. But the reading audience may see each word separately and have to de-process them after they reach the final noun. Compound adjectives without hyphens leave too much work for the reader; consider the following two examples from Michael Adams' *The Writer's Mind*:

```
dirty book burner
large scale fish investigation
```

Did a dirty person burn books? Or did someone burn dirty books? We cannot tell until the author tells us, with the addition of a hyphen. Are many authorities launching a huge investigation of scale fish? Is someone investigating large-scale fish? Or is the fish investigation large scale?

Most examples are less amusing; so is the confusion they create. A letter writer who recently requested a "temporary surface storage facility" may have been searching for a building with a temporary surface (paper, plastic) that is used for storing material. At the same time, the reader of the request letter might search the Yellow Pages for a building that stores surfaces, whatever that might be. A simple hyphen cures many of the phrase's ambiguities (replacing 'facility' with a more descriptive noun would help, too).

Some noun strings are easy to unravel; they merely distract us:

```
short term fringe benefits
present large power rate
a year round water supply
a gross receipts tax total
a much needed global analysis
```

```
the largest revenue producing center
the federal deposit insurance fund
high density nuclear waste
orbital transfer vehicle
long term permanent survival rate
cost containment move
```

Parenthetically, words that end with *ly* do not take a hyphen when used as compound adjectives; "duly noticed conference" contains within its *ly* the cue that one word has become an adverb modifying the following adjective. Readers can assimilate the *ly* unit quickly and correctly, as you, for instance, should be able to skim the following units:

```
newly financed system
hotly disputed divorce
financially secure widow
```

BREAKING UP UNITS

Many noun strings are problematic both because of the ambiguity that results from faulty punctuation and because of the excessive lengths of the noun strings. The more experience legal writers have in a specific area of the law, the more difficult it is for them to identify and change these strings. Long-distance telephone-company officials, for instance, might write "local exchange companies' access service devices" because they work with telecommunications and know the different local exchange companies. They know that these companies need services, and one of the services has something to do with access. This six-word string could not be simpler to those in that field. But what happens if an inventor asks a search team to investigate patents for his "local exchange companies' access service devices"? He would probably get reports on all sorts of devices, including some for local exchanges, for exchange companies, for access service, and for companies' access. Readers cannot tell which words belong with which unit; familiarity on the part of the writer creates confusion for the readers.

What, for instance, is a "first mortgage bond insurance capacity"? The writer of this noun string deals with bonds all day, and that entire unit of words flashes a concrete image across his mental screen. The rest of us still have a blank screen or a fuzzy one. We do not have the tools to help us focus on the entity; we cannot distinguish the main noun (capacity) from its modifiers. We need at least a hyphen or two here.

Better yet, the writer could replace "capacity" or unstring the line of qualifiers and add glue words to signal the relationship of the parts.

If you were able to follow the above example because you recognized the underlying meaning of the phrase, you might switch to a different subject matter for a small challenge: of a health policy, an employee recently wrote his employer asking, "Is the insurer saying that no significantly lasting objective treatment benefit can be assured?" Indeed! Perhaps the insured and insurer both skipped along anticipating the noun "benefit"; I assumed the first unit of thought concluded with "treatment" but then could not assimilate the final noun. The string was too long and contained too many abstract words. Adding signal words and hyphens, the author might rewrite, "Is the insurer saying the company cannot be assured that the benefit of the objective treatment will be long lasting, so they will not insure the treatment?" The rewrite is longer, obviously, and still mushy in the parts where I cannot even guess the intended meaning, but at least it now divides into processable units.

Some words are written as compound adjectives so frequently that they develop within our vernacular into a single word. For example, we used to have machines that interpreted information. That led to "data processing," a noun, and then the adjective: "data-processing" machine. The combination requires a hyphen to reflect its status as a compound adjective, and today it is frequently written as one word: "dataprocessing" machines. Similarly, a housing project, designed for many people, was "multi-family" housing, and now is "multifamily" housing. Similarly, prefixes, when used consistently with another adjective before a noun, also transform into new words: a "pre-hearing" conference is now a "prehearing" conference.

An irony is obvious: the more experience you have in your legal area, the more likely you will create and repeat noun strings. The more knowledge you possess, the bigger chance of confusing your readers. For documents written to the inexperienced, the experienced writer must edit with fresh eyes or ask someone else to review the prose.

VI
ADVICE AND
REFERENCES
So Go Be an Expert

Even expert writers review basic rules occasionally. Correcting their own writing is difficult because, as the creators, they cannot easily recognize what they have done wrong.

27
TESTING YOUR BASICS

The following ten sentences contain common errors; if you pit yourself against the grammar books here for a moment, you can identify your own problem areas and better know where to self-edit. If you recognize the problem in eight or more of the examples, you obviously have little trouble with sentence-level constructions. Five to seven correct answers reflect a typical need for a good desktop grammar book—dog-eared to your weak spots. A score below five may convince you to enroll in a night class for feedback about writing problems.

QUIZ

Correct the errors in the following sentences:

1. I do not object to him testifying about the sequence of events.
2. Prosecutor to witness: Is it not true that the sun rises in the east?
   Witness: Yes.
3. As a freshman, I studied property, the history of Anglo-Saxon paranoia, civil procedure, a class with the Erie Railroad running throughout, contracts, a course in the meaning of ambiguous words, and torts, the only subject any of us could imagine applicable to the real world.

4. Hopefully, I will be able to conclude this argument by Friday.

5. The victim in addition to her family and friends
   are insisting on a dismissal.

6. The police only told me yesterday that there was
   additional information.

7. I will give the brief to whomever asks for it
   first.

8. None of the summer clerks in the Ohio law firms are
   confident that they will receive a job offer.

9. Rejecting the summary of the leading case, the
   brief was judged inaccurate by the research
   attorney.

10. Because of scheduling problems, Kurt turned over
    the case to Bob and myself.

DISCUSSION

1. *I do not object to his testifying about the sequence of events.* Before a gerund (an *-ing* verb used as a noun), pronouns take the possessive. If the writer wanted to object to the man himself, who happened to be testifying, then the sentence written "object to him, testifying" would have been correct with the *-ing* verb used as a verbal participle. But the writer meant that she objected to the testimony, so "testifying" is a noun and the object of the preposition "to"; its modification is therefore an adjective, a possessive pronoun.

2. *Yes, what?* The use of the negative in the question presents a dilemma: what does the prosecutor want the witness to admit? Without the "not," the witness is asked, "Is it true that . . . ." The witness' original answer would then be correct. With the complicating negative, the hapless witness has no choice but to incorrectly respond to the English idiom with either "yes" or "no." People confronted with these negatives in conversation usually add explanatory phrases: "Yes, the sun rises in the east."

An attorney from Sugar Land submitted this example from a recent case: the witness muddled through with "no," allowing the participants to refer later to that "negative" answer. To avoid the confusion that the "is it not true" construction creates, attorneys would do well to convert the sentence into the positive. "Do you not agree that" presents the same dilemma.

3. *As a freshman, I studied property, the history of Anglo-Saxon paranoia; civil procedure, a class with the Erie Railroad running*

throughout; contracts, a course in the meaning of ambiguous words; and torts, the only subject any of us could imagine applicable to the real world. Commas separate equal ideas in a series, and they can also introduce qualifying phrases. But those small commas cannot perform both functions within the same sentence without miscueing readers. To signal the difference between the list and its qualifications, a writer can substitute semicolons for serial commas.

Notice that a semicolon before the *and* in the series creates a visual break before the final item and emphasizes the equality of the four courses.

4. *I hope to conclude this argument by Friday.* Traditionally, *hopefully* was used only as an adverb and thus had to modify the verb, or an adjective or adverb in the sentence. Thus a traditional interpretation of this sentence is "I will conclude this argument by Friday with a note of hope" or perhaps "I will be able to conclude with hope this article by Friday."

5. *The victim in addition to her family and friends is insisting on a dismissal.* Prepositional phrases between the subject and verb do not affect the relationship of the subject and verb. These intervening phrases can be labeled "qualifiers," if that helps writers remember the subject-verb agreement rule. Another example may help clarify the point: "He, like me, is planning a long vacation."

6. *The police told me only yesterday that there was additional information.* The misplaced *only* emphasizes *told* and suggests that the police could have hinted earlier, or that they *told* rather than explained.

7. *I will give the brief to whoever asks for it first.* Pronouns are inflected depending on placement and purpose. Pronouns take the case of the noun they are substitutes for, and thus this example needs a subjective pronoun to form the subject of the internal clause, "whoever asks for it first." This sentence is complicated by the clause's position in the sentence as the object of the preposition "to." If a noun or pronoun is both the subject of an internal clause and the object of the larger clause, then the internal clause dominates and must be made whole before the rest of the sentence is parsed.

8. *None of the summer law clerks in the Ohio law firm is confident that any of them will receive a job offer.* Traditionally, *none* takes a singular verb because the word means "not a single one." If you read this sentence with that definition, you will see that "Not one of the summer clerks is confident" presents the correct subject-verb agreement. However, some grammarians today argue that *none* can be singular or plural depending on context: "Are none of the clerks women?" sounds correct in conversation, but to write that question requires two shifts

from the formal construction: "Is not one of these clerks a woman?" Once we switch the meaning from singular to plural and adjust the verb, we also have to change "a woman" to "women." Because spoken English and written English vary in these important ways, "None of the grammarians today agree on the best solution to the conflict."

An interesting question here is the amount of colloquial language that writers will allow in their legal work. Some writers are uncomfortable with "none are" but accept the contraction "aren't I" rather than "am't I" ("Are I not" rather than the correct "Am I not").

9. *Rejecting the summary of the leading case, the research attorney judged the brief was inaccurate.* In the original sentence, the introductory verbal (-*ing* verb) does not clearly point to the noun it modifies. Placed next to the original noun/subject, the phrase modified "brief," implying that the brief was rejecting its own summary. By shifting the sentence from passive to active voice and moving the agent ("research attorney") near the introductory phrase, the writer can avoid ambiguity and, in this case, the embarrassment of being taken literally.

10. *Because of scheduling problems, Kurt turned over the case to Bob and me.* A pronoun following a preposition belongs in the objective case (*me, you, him, her, it, us, them*). *Myself* is in the reflexive case, which is used to intensify ("I would rather do it myself") or to indicate a reflexive action, when the subject of the sentence is also the object of the verb ("The attorneys talked themselves into a corner").

28

GRAMMAR RULES VERSUS SUGGESTIONS

Back when we were taught the rules of our language, we were also indoctrinated with a group of suggestions from well-meaning teachers who were tired of students' sentence fragments or stream-of-consciousness prose. To help students avoid fragments, for instance, grammar school teachers offer up certain "rules" that guide students toward more sophisticated writing. Unfortunately, these bits of advice become "the law" and remain "the law" long after they have served their useful purpose.

Other bits of "rules" have their origins in foreign languages; teachers who have studied classical languages want to keep our language as pure as some idealized language, usually Latin, but occasionally even Greek. Fortunately, language teachers in this decade have conceded that what was essential for Romans speaking their own Latin may not be necessary for Americans speaking English.

GRAMMAR-RULE MYTHS

Below is a list of stylistic options that have been mislabeled as rules. If you worry that your audience believes these are rules or that your audience would perceive any of these stylistic devices as patronizing, offensive, or overly casual, then you will of course elect to not use them.

You cannot write a one-sentence paragraph.

Why not?

This myth probably began with elementary school teachers who despaired of reading one-sentence paragraphs from thirty young students. Declaring an arbitrary "rule" for fifth graders allows teachers to concentrate on paragraph development, topic sentences, and organization. That an occasional one-sentence paragraph is legitimate simply is not discussed. But we are no longer in the fifth grade—as adults we are no longer required to heed that prohibition.

Sophisticated writers use one-sentence paragraphs for deliberate strategy. Creative writers make excellent use of one-sentence paragraphs to form natural transitions between two major points, or to create emphasis. Legal writers can too. Perhaps if legal writers produced long documents containing *only* one-sentence paragraphs, then their writing would be judged as elementary and undeveloped. But legal writers are rarely so inclined. Today you may use occasional, deliberate one-sentence paragraphs and not feel guilty.

You cannot begin a sentence with <u>and</u> or <u>but</u>.

These conjunctions serve as perfectly valid beginnings for a sentence—and do so in many novels, poems, and essays. Used sparingly, they call the readers' attention to added information ("And the defendant never replied.") or to contradictory information ("But the defendant never replied.").

This "rule" enters our lives around the third grade, when teachers tire of state-flower reports that read, "Texas' state flower is the bluebonnet. And bluebonnet tells the color. And the shape. And so I picked it." A rule against *and* and *but* eliminates both the fragment and the singsong cadence.

Excessive coordination is natural to our linguistic development—when we first talk, we string ideas together with *and*s; when we begin writing, we mimic our speech pattern. The novice's reliance on coordination produces monotonous syntax and eventually sentence error, like the sentence fragment in the grammar school example above. Determined to save us from the pits of prose hell (e.g., sentence fragments), our well-meaning teachers create "rules." But we are no longer in elementary school, and attorneys rarely produce inadvertent sentence fragments, so you should feel free to deliberately begin with *and* and *but*.

But, you argue, beginning sentences with conjunctions could create jumbled, disconnected prose. The conjunctions, to the contrary, provide emphasis, surprise, and interest. Even H. W. Fowler, in his 1965 *A Dictionary of Modern English Usage*, determined that the ironclad decision to avoid introductory conjunctions was a "faintly lingering superstition." [1] Surely we can let go today.

You cannot begin a sentence with <u>however</u>.

However is a conjunctive adjective that connects two ideas and is used as a transition meaning "in spite of that," "but," or "on the other hand." It should be placed to emphasize the sentence element being contrasted. That means it might necessarily precede the subject, or the verb, or even the object of the sentence, depending on the writer's chosen emphasis:

> In Texas, state trial judges are not prohibited from participating in the plea bargaining process. Their involvement must not be so great, <u>however</u>, as to render a guilty plea involuntary.
>
> He claims the psychiatrist contradicted himself during the competency hearing. <u>However</u>, the hearing's records prove him wrong.
>
> The CLE committee scheduled a conference in Miami. A hurricane, <u>however</u>, changed the course of events.

A dissenting vote on the freedom of *however* is cast by William Strunk, Jr., and E. B. White in *The Elements of Style*. They maintain that *however*, if used to mean *nevertheless*, serves better when not in the first position.[2] Unfortunately, they do not explain why they believe even *nevertheless* should be buried elsewhere in the sentence. Perhaps it is because Professor Strunk disliked the sound of the word: In the introduction, editor White said of his teacher, "[Strunk] had a number of likes and dislikes that were almost as whimsical as the choice of a necktie, yet he made them seem utterly convincing." [3] Some Strunk and White readers are indeed convinced, but surely not by the logic of the rule—perhaps by its relationship to Latin syntax.

———

[1] H. W. FOWLER, A DICTIONARY OF MODERN ENGLISH USAGE 29 (Ernest Gowers rev., 2d ed. 1965).
[2] WILLIAM STRUNK, JR., & E. B. WHITE, THE ELEMENTS OF STYLE 48 (3d ed. 1979).
[3] *Id.* at xv.

Traditionalists attempt to follow Latin or Greek syntax in which a sentence beginning with a conjunctive adverb is unusual. English does not follow Latin syntax, does not decline or necessarily conjugate, and does not have much in common with Greek except for prefixes, suffixes, and some vocabulary. English speakers are free to use *however* in any position that emphasizes the sentence element they want emphasized.

Avoid first-person and second-person pronouns.

I am surprised at the number of writers who would write a convoluted sentence, distancing the writer and reader, rather than use even one first-person pronoun:

```
Of the above options, a sellout is the only logi-
cal conclusion that one can recommend. Therefore,
a sellout is recommended for XYZ Corporation.
```

Using *one* in the first sentence pushed the second sentence into an ambiguous passive voice. The same type of writers avoid the second person:

```
The effect of the new bill on the reader will
depend on income and his tax bracket.
```

The only excuse for this kind of distancing is a law review article, in which active voice is déclassé, or a government agency opinion that is meant to apply to a wider audience than the purported original audience. Notice that writing "the reader" instead of "you" in the above example forced the writer to use the third-person singular pronoun "his," which adds the "his/her" stylistic dilemma to what might have been a straightforward sentence: The effect of the new bill on *you* will depend on income and *your* tax bracket.

Of course, the first-person pronoun is inappropriate at times: a legal opinion issued from the state comptroller's office would create questions and criticism if the auditor wrote: "I am holding you responsible for three years of back taxes on your state-based operations." The writer is obviously not the entity pointing a finger at the reader; the agency is, and the first-person pronoun is inappropriate.

If you mean "I," though, use "I." It is not automatically wrong. Some teachers have argued, for instance, that letter-writers should *never* begin paragraphs with "I," because the reader would believe the writer was self-centered and egotistical. Maybe novice writers have misinterpreted that suggestion by Miss Manners as a rule for all letter writers. It is not. Nor is it a rule for other formats. Rather than convolute a sentence just to avoid first person, consider the audience and the purpose of the document. If a memorandum is to be read by your supervising attorney, you may comfortably use "I" in your concluding recommendation to signal that you have reached a point of closure, of summary. If that summary is later incorporated into a brief, then you should return to the conclusion and replace both the pronoun and the sentiment of the recommendation.

Never end a sentence with a preposition.

Not true. Although *preposition* derives from a Latin word meaning "to place in front," English terminology frequently requires a concluding preposition.

```
This is a serious matter that ought to be in-
quired into.
```

Winston Churchill purportedly told a young editor who had circled Churchill's conclusory prepositions, "That is an absurdity up with which I will not put." And that is the position most grammarians end up with.

On the other hand, repetitious prepositions at the ends of sentences create a problem, exemplified by the familiar Aggie joke, "Where's the library at?" The "at" is not merely misplaced at the end of the sentence, as the joke would have us believe; the "at" creates redundancy because the adverb already signals the question.

Never split an infinitive.

Not true. Most foreign languages cannot split their infinitives (*andar, escribir*), but luckily English allows this variation of order so that the sentence can follow the normal rhythm of English sentences. To move an adverb around just to avoid the infinitive can create patent artificiality. There is no "rule" in English about split infinitives—just the common-sense suggestion that adverbs should be placed where they sound best. Writers need to listen to their own sentences and avoid the distortions that can result from strict adherence to a nonrule:

```
"To really understand the law" [split infini-
tive] or
"Really to understand the law"
```

Even traditional grammarians, who may not find split infinitives desirable, don't uniformly condemn them, because the alternative may create a real ambiguity. Look at the following examples from Fowler's *Modern English Usage*:

```
   Both Germany and England have done ill in not
combining to forbid flatly hostilities.
   Safeguards should be provided to prevent effec-
tually cosmopolitan financiers from manipulating
these reserves.4
```

Common sense tells us that these sentences need to be rearranged so that the adverbs are not "squinting," modifying both the word in front and the word behind them. If the adverb could be interpreted to modify the word after it as well as the verb before it, then careful writers need to split the infinitive to avoid the possible ambiguity.

CONCLUSION

Grammar rules, like punctuation rules, were developed to help writers avoid ambiguity and confusion. Stylistic suggestions were developed to help writers produce more graceful, more memorable, more persuasive prose. If a suggestion helps you avoid ambiguity and confusion, use the suggestion. If the suggestion results in artifice for its own sake, or creates the opportunity for ambiguity, or keeps you from being persuasive, then that suggestion is not one you should be bound by. They're dicta.

---

4 FOWLER, *supra* note 1, at 580–581.

- I can't figure out what he wants.
- They've never explained what they expect me to do, but they keep returning my work edited to pieces.
- Every associate who has worked for him in the last four years has left the firm.

29
ADVICE TO PARTNERS ABOUT ADVICE

Partners may not be aware that they have any effect on the quality of the work they will read in the future. Nevertheless, top management sets the standard in most law firms, through both explicit and implicit attitudes toward the value of writing. The problem is that partners can undercut their explicit, positive statements with implicit and negative gestures about writing. That is, while they are saying "Of course this firm depends on writing abilities—that's how we are judged by the community," these same partners undercut their message with implicit gestures, which can be labeled as sins of both omission and commission.

By engaging in implicit sins of *omission*, partners are not actually asking for bad writing. Rather, they ignore both the writing process and the opportunity to help their associates by providing feedback. Sins of *commission* are perhaps even more deadly to office morale and thus the reputation of the law firm. These sins place the partners and associates on a path of predictably bad writing by destroying their associates' developing writing talents and by imposing their own dogmatic standards on the apprentice associates. A partner who makes excessive changes in every associate's work, who gives blanket rejections and ambiguous advice, or who pressures the associates to adopt his writing style is on a messianic mission that undermines the writing talents of the associates by failing to allow them to develop along different (and perhaps better) paths.

The negative traits of some partners undermine the realistic and professional goals they may explicitly express. The following list allows you a different perspective on partners' character traits. The list may hit an exposed nerve; my intent is to provide a light view of the techniques some partners inadvertently employ that can nevertheless undermine a law firm's writing performance. Here, then, are ways you can develop into an obstructive and defeating supervising partner.

HOW A PARTNER SINS: OMISSION

Function as an unintentional bad example.

Never change your own writing style, even if someone takes the time and has the patience to point out your problems. If an associate presumes to offer advice, of course you will have to appear to welcome it and seem to listen. But as a partner, you know that you already have an excellent style. How else would you have made partner? Do not ever take advice: pretend to misunderstand subtle hints. After working for you daily, your associates will begin emulating this technique.

Assume that if a document is given to you, it is ready to go.

As supervising partner, you will want to make sure that the associate does not completely miss the legal issue, but otherwise you should send the document out without fussing over it. Do not waste your time changing things; similarly, do not give associates any feedback. After all, they are busy researching and writing—doing what they were hired to do. They do not need for you to take up their time on itty-bitty details like writing. Besides, no one has ever explained to a supervising partner *how* to critique an associate's writing, and you would not want to offer incorrect advice. If associates dare to ask for feedback, either ignore them or put them off: "We'll talk about your memo [or brief or contract] writing during your annual review." Then your associates do not have to fret, wasting energy on writing style when they need to concentrate on the law instead.

Tout oral advocacy and ignore writing problems.

This technique has worked in law schools for generations. If associates have obvious writing problems, do not suggest that they seek outside help. Rather, brag about their speaking ability and remind them that electronic media are replacing written communications. After all, the telephone will soon replace the letter. And judges do not read briefs anyway—they just accept their clerks' advice before the oral arguments.

HOW A PARTNER SINS: COMMISSION

Double-question every word on memoranda.

When an associate gives you a document for review, take out the old red pen and strike through half the words and ideas. Ask a question about each paragraph—no matter how simple the idea it contains. Thus your advice for essential surgery will get jumbled with cosmetic suggestions so that important writing problems are equated with your personal stylistic whims. A sly trick here is to change all the associate's words but end up with a memorandum that says the same as the original—just all in your own words. That will teach associates that the quality of their original work does not matter—you are just going to rewrite it anyway.

Give ambiguous blanket rejections.

Throw the memorandum back and insist on a rewrite. But under no circumstances should you relent and admit what needs to be changed (that would be spoon-feeding). As the supervising partner, though, do continue to remind associates—at firm-wide events if possible—of your deep concern about their writing abilities and warn them that unless their style improves, you will not be able to recommend that they stay with the firm.

Sneak in ambiguous revisions.

Allow the associate to submit the document, but offer no feedback; later, surreptitiously allow the associate to see the final version, in which you have drastically changed words, phrases, and entire case interpretations. To make this editing technique effective, you cannot allow any opening for an associate to question your changes. Your associates' predictable responses to this shotgun approach will be capitulation; they simply pass you their drafts instead of polished writing.

Belabor a pet peeve.

Hook onto a single theme or phrase or even an old high school rule you think you remember, and always comment on its misuse. To make this technique effective, you will ignore the more important aspects of the associate's writing, because naturally you do not have time to focus on everything.

Expect too much, too soon.

Keep the golden age philosophy: "Why, when I was a new associate, I wrote ten memos and a complex brief the first month—and did my own bookkeeping." Assume that first-year associates know the background of every legal issue—that is why they went to law school, isn't it? Therefore, you can feel free to cut by half the time that the associates estimate it will take to complete the work. If the associates catch on to this technique, try a variant: change the announced deadline to "tomorrow" and keep those youngsters on their toes. That way the associates will always know they have not turned in their best work and will not be ego-involved in its outcome.

SOLUTIONS: PARTNERS HELP ASSOCIATES

Implicit attitudes are difficult to change. If you feel that the above descriptions are too familiar for comfort, you can always get help—either psychological help or editing help. My purpose for providing the following editing suggestions is to remind the supervising partner that behind every memorandum is an associate who needs a thoughtful critique that he or she can accept and integrate into future writings. Just as partners have egos, so, too, do associates who easily feel slighted if their work never receives any feedback. And, being human, associates become defensive in response to blanket criticisms about their writing abilities. A perceptive partner works to keep personal judgments from developing into an argument or bloodbath and uses a critique session as a part of the firm's educational programs.

Below, I offer a few editing tips to help you on your way. They help me when I am judging a writer's ability or when I am editing a document (two very different functions). Supervising partners may want to adopt a few of these ideas to help them become more professional and thus elicit more positive results:

1. Narrow responses to what the author has asked you to check: length? grammar? organization? rhetorical effect? If an author asks me for help but has no idea what kind of help, I try to limit my written comments to the essentials. A page covered with editorial ink does not help anyone improve anything.

2. If simply everything about the author's prose style is terrible, limit comments to the one area that could produce the most noticeable results. Usually organization and transitional cues prove the most useful for isolated emphasis; if the author can correct problems in these areas, another reader should at least understand the line of analysis and what

the reader is supposed to do about it. Only when weak writers can solve these first two problems can they address other incorrect or distracting elements of style.

3. Ask a question rather than give an answer. "Are you hoping the judge will ignore this case because you've placed it back here?" or "Do you think this long section could benefit from subheads?" The questions engage the associates in a dialogue and allow them to incorporate your suggestion with the answer. For instance, you might be tempted to say, "Your conclusion doesn't have anything to do with your analysis." However, asking a question can elicit a more thoughtful and useful response: "I'm lost. How does your conclusion follow what you describe about the precedent case?"

4. Identify pet peeves for what they are. At the end of a critique session, I usually conclude: "We've discussed the writing habits that might cause you trouble. Now let me show you a few of my own pet peeves, writing habits that I find really distracting. They don't break any rules, and perhaps other readers wouldn't react against them, but you might want to consider them and see if they are worth changing."

5. Create a written evaluation form that the associates can take away from the session. At the privacy of their desks, the associates can more calmly review summaries of strengths and weaknesses. Without the written conclusion, associates may forget the praiseworthy aspects of their written work and concentrate on the criticisms, which could prove detrimental to both the associates and the firm. These evaluation forms do not have to be time consuming or complicated. I am providing a sample form that may be cut or expanded but can get you started.

PARTNERS HELP THEMSELVES

A supervising partner affects the attitudes of the associates and thus their products. If a partner knows she is exhibiting any of the negative traits above, only she can decide to change them, and that can happen only when she confronts the causes. If a partner's writing style is bad, that failing will lead to insecurity—lawyers are indeed judged by their abilities to communicate. No one can hide this inadequacy for very long, not even senior partners. And, not infrequently, insecurities lead to the negative defense traits I have listed above. If partners decide they have been unusually negative to associates' writing because of this problem, perhaps they should seek editing advice for themselves. It is an unfortunate reality that none of us enjoys focusing on our deficiencies, especially if

Sample Evaluation Form

[Note to supervising partner: Use this simplified form to evaluate the written work of your associates. Each category is separate and should not influence another. Please feel free to expand your evaluation beyond the questions in this form.]

Analysis and Research

_____ Relevant issues identified and weighed

_____ Research thorough and complete

_____ Sound analysis

_____ Conclusion justified

Style

_____ Introduction and conclusion useful for quick scanning

_____ Sentence and paragraph length appropriate and readable

_____ Vocabulary (and jargon) appropriate for intended audience

_____ Mechanics (grammar, spelling, punctuation) clear and precise, needing only minor editing

Ratings

1. *Superior.* Excels in this aspect of writing and is more skilled than most members of the firm. (Approximately 5 percent of associates may receive this rating.)
2. *Competent.* Comparable to all other good writers in the firm, with a few (correctable) problems. Good work. (Approximately 85 percent of associates receive this rating in a strong law firm.)
3. *Weak in this area.* Associate needs to concentrate on this area and overcome deficiencies to match the firm's expectations. (Approximately 10 percent of associates in a strong law firm, but up to 50 percent if associates have not had enough writing experience, receive this rating.)

Additional Comments:

we have functioned without ever having confronted them. And partners in law firms have even more reason to retain the status quo than most writers: partners are already fairly successful, every moment of their time is committed until somewhere in 1999, and the world at large assumes lawyers already know how to write competently (although maybe obscurely). So a partner's asking for help will occur only if "something happens"—a public reprimand or ridicule, an anonymous office note that hits the mark, or, on the more positive side, the partner's decision to improve that weak area of his professionalism.

Once the decision is made, though, partners must look for help: they can study books about (legal) writing, or they can ask knowledgeable relatives or friends for aid. Another source of help for weak writers is an outside professional, someone who evaluates and offers suggestions without any personal involvement. An additional plus to the professional editor is just that—"professional" should mean that the editor is familiar with a professional's writing tasks and can confidently (and confidentially) evaluate prose for specific problems, like too-dense prose or repetitive topic sentences. Under the guidance of an editor, partners can concurrently investigate their own weaknesses and learn professional editing techniques.

If weak writers cannot bring themselves to get help to overcome these writing insecurities, the cycle of bad writing will be handed down through the generations within the law firm. Associates learn from partners. Partners who fail to recognize that they are suppressing good writers risk losing the opportunity to develop the firm's collective writing reputation. And, by discouraging this important aspect of professionalism, the partner will keep the firm from becoming the competitive law firm he or she wanted to build.

30
REFERENCE BOOKS
FOR LEGAL WRITERS

I am a reference-book collector. Please take this admission with the same solemnity that you reserve for other confessions: "Hi, I'm Joe, and I am an alcoholic," or "Yes, let's have lunch, but I'm diabetic and vegetarian." Reference-book collecting can signal a problem. My collection of reference books threatens to push me out of the office; it oozes from under my bed and lines the stairs to my study. I open these books while people are trying to talk with me on the telephone. I thumb through reference books while students explain why they turned in a brief after the deadline. I carry two paperback reference books in my briefcase so I have something to read in airports. Never have I thrown away a good old reference book. I have replaced them. Once I tried looking up the spelling of one of those *-able*, *-ible* words and discovered that my faithful dictionary did not organize troubling words that way. Investigating the copyright date, I remembered that I had received "old faithful" the day I graduated from high school—in 1964. My elusive word probably had not been invented in 1964. Off I trotted to the bookstore and indulged in a little set of three references, cleverly packaged in a box that sits on my desk. In the box are a new(er) pocket dictionary, a thesaurus, and a dictionary of synonyms. The box works as a bookend for papers on my desk, and I use all three small books daily. But "old faithful" is behind me on the shelf. Who knows when I will need a more comprehensive collection?

Writers can buy the books that promise to answer their most conscious questions; they can borrow reference books from friends and copy snippets of useful advice. Really good friends, I think, give reference books to each other at Christmas and for birthdays or even to say "thank you." They last longer than flowers or wine and prove that you know just what your friend would like to read about.

So here are my suggestions for writers who want to improve their writing skills—or who believe a friend of theirs does. If you are in need of a small but complete reference book about writing in general, I suggest either *The St. Martin's Handbook* (traditional textbook) or Joseph Williams' *Style: Ten Lessons in Clarity and Grace* (short, readable essays on prose style).

If you want to examine more fully the particulars of specific drafting techniques, for instance, horizontal and vertical checks or the intricacies of parallelism in drafting, investigate Reed Dickerson's collection of articles in *Materials on Legal Drafting*.

GENERAL WRITING ADVICE

- *Adams, Michael. *The Writer's Mind*. Glenview, Ill.: Scott, Foresman, 1984.
- Barzun, Jacques. *Simple and Direct*. New York: Harper & Row, 1985.
- Bernstein, Theodore M. *The Careful Writer: A Modern Guide to English Usage*. New York: Atheneum, 1965.
- ———. *Miss Thistlebottom's Hobgoblins: The Careful Writer's Guide to the Taboos, Bugbears and Outmoded Rules of English Usage*. New York: Simon & Schuster, 1971.
- Corder, Jim, and John Ruszkiewitz. *Handbook of Current English*. Glenview, Ill.: Scott, Foresman, 1989.
- Dickson, Paul. *Words: A Connoisseur's Collection of Old and New, Weird and Wonderful, Useful and Outlandish*. New York: Dell Publishing Co., 1982.
- Flower, Linda. *Problem-Solving Strategies for Writing*. New York: Harcourt Brace Jovanovich, 1981.
- Follett, Wilson. *Modern American Usage: A Guide*. Edited and completed by Jacques Barzun et al. New York: Hill & Wang, 1966.

---

* Highly recommended.

- Fowler, H. W. *A Dictionary of Modern English Usage.* 2d ed. Revised by Sir Ernest Gowers. New York: Oxford University Press, 1965.
- Goldberg, Natalie. *Writing Down the Bones.* Boston: Shambhala Publishing Co., 1982.
- Gordon, Karen Elizabeth. *The Transitive Vampire.* New York: Times Books, 1984.
- ———. *The Well-Tempered Sentence.* New York: Ticknor & Fields, 1983.
- Jacobi, Ernst. *Writing at Work: Dos, Don'ts and How Tos.* Rochelle Park, N.J.: Hayden Book Co., 1979.
- Kerrigan, William. *Writing to the Point: Six Basic Steps.* New York: Harcourt Brace Jovanovich, 1974.
- Patrick, J. Max, and Robert O. Evans, eds., *Style, Rhetoric, and Rhythm.* Princeton, N.J.: Princeton University Press, 1966.
- Rico, Gabriele Lusser. *Writing the Natural Way: Using Right-Brain Techniques to Release Your Expressive Power.* Los Angeles: J. P. Tarcher, 1983.
- Sabin, William. *Gregg Reference Manual.* New York: McGraw-Hill, 1985.
- Safire, William. *On Language.* New York: Times Books, 1982.
- ———. *What's the Good Word?* New York: Avon Books, 1982.
- Safire, William, and Leonard Safir. *Good Advice.* New York: Times Books, 1984.
- **The St. Martin's Handbook.* Edited by Andrea Lunsford and Robert Connors. New York: St. Martin's Press, 1992.
- Sandell, Rolf. *Linguistic Style and Persuasion.* San Francisco: Academic Press, 1977.
- Strunk, William, Jr., and E. B. White. *The Elements of Style.* 3d ed. New York: Macmillan, 1979.
- Tortoriello, Thomas; Stephen Blatt; and Sue DeWine. *Communication in the Organization: An Applied Approach.* New York: McGraw-Hill Co., 1978.
- Trimble, John R. *Writing with Style.* Englewood Cliffs, N.J.: Prentice-Hall, 1975.
- U.S. Government Printing Office. *A Manual of Style.* New York; Crown Publishing Co., 1986.

▄▄▄

* Highly recommended.

- Venolia, Jan. *Write Right!* Berkeley: Ten Speed Press, 1982.
- * Williams, Joseph. *Style: Ten Lessons in Clarity and Grace.* New York: Scott, Foresman, 1985.

LEGAL WRITING ADVICE

- * Aldisert, Ruggero. *Logic for Lawyers.* New York: Clark Boardman, 1989.
- Benson, Robert, and Joan Kessler. "Legalese v. Plain English: An Empirical Study of Persuasion and Credibility in Appellate Brief Writing." 20 *Loyola of Los Angeles Law Review* 301 (1987).
- Biskind, Elliot. *Legal Writing Simplified.* New York: Clark Boardman Co., 1971.
- Bloss, Julie. "How to Review a Contract." 91 *Case & Comment* 38 (1986).
- Brody, Susan, et al. *Legal Drafting.* Boston: Little, Brown, & Co., 1994.
- Burnham, Scott. *Drafting Contracts.* Charlottesville, N.C.: Michie Co., 1987.
- California Continuing Education of the Bar. *How to Draft Wills.* Berkeley: California Continuing Education of the Bar, 1985.
- Child, Barbara. *Drafting Legal Documents: Materials and Problems.* St. Paul, Minn.: West Publishing Co., 1988.
- Cooper, Frank. *Writing in Law Practice.* Indianapolis, Ind.: Bobbs-Merrill Co., 1963.
- Crump, David. "The Five Elements of a Contract: Avoiding Ambiguity in Them." 43 *Texas Bar Journal* 370 (1980).
- Cuff, Terence. "Drafting Agreements." 15 *Barrister* 41 (Winter 1988).
- Cusack, Lawrence. "The Blue Pencilled Will: What's Wrong with a Will in Plain English?" 118 *Trusts & Estates* 33 (1979).
- * Dickerson, Reed. *The Fundamentals of Legal Drafting.* 2d ed. Boston: Little, Brown, 1986.
- ———. "How to Write a Law." 31 *Notre Dame Lawyer* 14 (1955).
- ———. *Legislative Drafting.* 2d ed. Boston: Little, Brown and Co., 2nd ed. 1977.

---

* Highly recommended.

- ———. *Materials on Legal Drafting*. New York: West Publishing Co., 1981.
- ———. "Plain English Statutes and Readability—Part 1." 64 *Michigan Bar Journal* 567 (1985).
- Dunahoo, Kermit. "Avoiding Inadvertent Syntactic Ambiguity in Legal Draftsmanship." 20 *Drake Law Review* 137 (1970).
- Felsenfeld, Carl, and Alan Siegel. *Writing Contracts in Plain English*. St. Paul, Minn.: West Publishing Co., 1981.
- Fidel, Noel. "Some Do's and Don'ts of Motion Writing." 19 *Arizona Bar Journal* 8 (1983).
- Flesch, Rudolf. *How to Write Plain English: A Book for Lawyers and Consumers*. New York: Harper & Row, 1979.
- Goldblatt, Michael. "Well-drafted Contracts Keep Client and You Out of Court: Here's How!" 7 *Preventive Law Reporter* 14 (1988).
- Goldfarb, Ronald, and James Raymond. *Clear Understandings*. New York: West Publishing Co., 1982.
- *Goldstein, Tom, and Jethro Leiberman. *The Lawyer's Guide to Writing Well*. Berkeley: University of California Press, 1991.
- * Good, C. Edward. *Mightier than the Sword: Powerful Writing in the Legal Profession*. Charlottesville, Va.: Blue Jeans Press, 1989.
- Goodwin, Rodney. "Drafting Buy-Sell Agreements to Protect Both Buyer and Seller." 17 *Taxation for Lawyers* 124 (1988).
- Gopen, George. "Let the Buyer in Ordinary Course of Business Beware: Suggestions for Revising the Price of the Uniform Commercial Code." 54 *University of Chicago Law Review* 1178 (1987).
- Hathaway, George. "The Plain English Movement in the Law, Past, Present, and Future." 35 *Michigan Bar Journal* 1236 (1985).
- Haynsworth, Harry. "How to Draft Clear and Concise Legal Documents." 31 *Practical Lawyer* 41 (1985).
- Hurd, Hollis. *Writing for Lawyers*. Pittsburgh, Pa.: Journal Broadcasting and Communications, 1982.
- Joslyn, Robert. "Use of Plain English in Drafting Wills and Trusts." 63 *Michigan Bar Journal* 612 (1984).

---

* Highly recommended.

- Kaplan, Lucille. "Writing That Persuades: No Quick Fix for the Advocate." 20 *Trial* 44 (1984).
- Kuzara, Christine. "Plain English in Legislative Drafting." 62 *Michigan Bar Journal* 980 (1983).
- Lankford, Jefferson. "How to Write and Argue Motions." 25 *Arizona Attorney* 24 (1989).
- Laurino, Louis. "Avoiding Will Construction Problems." 11 *ALI-ABA Course Materials Journal* 83 (1987).
- LeClercq, Terri. "The Craft of Successful Drafting." *Texas Bar Journal* 1248 (1991).
- ———. *Guide to Legal Writing*. Boston: Little, Brown & Co., 1995.
- Llewellyn, Karl. "Remarks on the Theory of Appellate Decision and the Rule of Canons About How Statutes Are to Be Construed, 3 *Vanderbilt Law Review* 395 (1950).
- McDonald, Daniel. *The Language of Argument*. New York: Harper and Row, 3d ed. 1980.
- Mandel, Richard. *The Preparation of Commercial Agreements*. New York: Practising Law Institute, 1978.
- Maxey, David. "Fundamentals of Draftsmanship—A Guide in Preparing Agreements." 19 *Law Notes* 87 (Summer 1983).
- * Mellinkoff, David. *The Language of the Law*. Boston: Little, Brown, 1963.
- ———. *Legal Writing: Sense and Nonsense*. New York: Scribner's Sons, 1982.
- Neubauer, Mark. "Check-the-Box Pleadings." 11 *Litigation* 28 (Winter 1985).
- Pearsall, Thomas. *How to Write for the World of Work*. 2d ed. New York: CBS College Publishing, 1982.
- Perry, et al., *Introduction to Drafting California Legal Instruments*. San Diego: Jenkins & Perry, 1983.
- Practising Law Institute. *Basic Will Drafting* New York, 1989.
- ———. *Drafting Commercial Agreements*. New York, 1992.
- ———. *Practical Will Drafting* New York, 1976.
- Pratt, Diana V. *Legal Writing: A Systematic Approach*. 2d ed. American Casebook Series. St. Paul, Minn.: West Publishing Co., 1993.

---

* Highly recommended.

- Ray, Mary Bernard. *Legal Writing: Getting It Written.* St. Paul, Minn.: West Publishing Co., 1987.
- Redish, Janice. *How to Write Regulations (and Other Legal Documents) in Clear English.* Washington, D.C.: American Institutes for Research, 1983.
- Saxon, Charles. "Computer-aided Drafting of Legal Documents." 1982 *American Bar Foundation Research Journal* 685.
- Schleifer, Nancy. "Complaint and Defensive Checklists." 61 *Florida Bar Journal* 23 (1987).
- Shaffer, Thomas. *The Planning and Drafting of Legal Wills and Trusts.* New York: Foundation Press, 1979.
- Shapo, Helene; Marilyn Walters; and Elizabeth Fagans. *Writing and Analysis in the Law.* Westbury, N.Y.: Foundation Press, 1989.
- Solan, Lawrence. *Language of Judges.* Chicago: University of Chicago Press, 1993.
- Spears, Franklin. "Presenting an Effective Appeal." 21 *Trial* 95 (1985).
- Squires, Lynn. "A Simple 'Simple' Will." 57 *Washington Law Review* 461 (1982).
- Statsky, William. *Legislative Analysis and Drafting.* 2d ed. Boston: Little, Brown and Co., 1977.
- Tebeaux, Elizabeth. *Design of Business Communications: The Process and the Product.* New York: Macmillan, 1990.
- *Texas Law Review Manual on Style.* 7th ed. Austin: Texas Law Review Association, 1992.
- Till, Paul, and Albert Gargiulo. *Contracts: The Move to Plain Language.* New York: AMACOM (American Management Associations), 1979.
- Woolever, Kristine. *Untangling the Law: Strategies for Legal Writers.* Belmont, Cal.: Wadsworth Publishing Co., 1987.
- Word, James. "A Brief for Plain English Wills and Trusts." 14 *University of Richmond Law Review* 471 (1980).
- Wydick, Richard. *Plain English for Lawyers.* Chapel Hill, N.C.: Carolina Academic Press, 1985.

INDEX